DIFFER ENTIATE TO DOMINATE

GLOBAL
PUBLISHING
G R O U P

Global Publishing Group
Australia • New Zealand • Singapore • America • London

"You want a great brand? **...it starts with a plan."**

Includes...
questionnaires,
practical exercises
& downloadable
worksheets

DIFFER ENTIATE
DOM TO INATE

THE 7 STEPS TO TRANSFORM YOUR
BUSINESS INTO A BRAND

PETER ENGELHARDT

First Edition 2017

Copyright © 2017 Peter Engelhardt

All rights are reserved. The material contained within this book is protected by copyright law, no part may be copied, reproduced, presented, stored, communicated or transmitted in any form by any means without prior written permission..

National Library of Australia
Cataloguing-in-Publication entry:

Creator: Engelhardt, Peter, author.

Title: Differentiate to Dominate: The 7 Steps to Transform Your Business into a Brand / Peter Engelhardt.

1st ed.
ISBN: 9781925288209 (paperback)

Branding (Marketing)
Success in business

Dewey Number: 658.827

Published by Global Publishing Group
PO Box 517 Mt Evelyn, Victoria 3796 Australia
Email info@GlobalPublishingGroup.com.au

Printed in China

For further information about orders:
Phone: +61 3 9739 4686 or Fax +61 3 8648 6871

For Mum, Dad, Mandy and Miet

Peter Engelhardt

Acknowledgements

As with any endeavour of this sort, there are many people I would like to acknowledge.

First and foremost, I want to thank my wife, Mandy, for allowing me to pursue my dreams. I don't think there is any greater gift one can give. I know it hasn't been easy living with the highs and lows, yet you continue to be the most loving, supportive, smart and beautiful woman I have ever met.

I want to thank my daughter, Miet, who thinks I'm a great support in her life, but it goes two ways! You are the most empathetic, pretty young woman I know and I'm so proud of what you've achieved already in your life.

I'd like to thank my mentor Darren Stephens; if it wasn't for you this book would never have been born.

Next, a huge thanks to my staff. Together we have created an online platform that is the first of its kind and has, and will continue, to educate and change many lives. Your visions, encouragement and years of support have taken it to a level I could never have done on my own. Hayley Reeson, you're the bomb, always challenging and pushing for the best. Tom Francis, you're the design legend, turning ideas into pictures that say a thousand words. Aaron Tusjak, the 'nothing's too hard' king of coding. And Gary King, the English legend who supports everybody.

A special thank-you to my Mum and Dad, Ruth and Daniel, brother Ron and sisters, Anette and Caaren, for their utmost love and encouragement.

And lastly, a huge thank-you to our publisher Global Publishing Group and to their awesome team, for your dedication and commitment to the book's success.

In one book it's not possible to give you everything you need to build an industry leading 'brand.' So I've created the **Plan2Brand online tool** so you can fast track your growth and success.

It's the world's only interactive platform that teaches you how to create a set of brand foundations and a brand strategy.

A STEP-BY-STEP PROGRAM FOR CREATING AND GROWING A SUCCESSFUL BRAND

Plan 2 Brand

Strategic planning, goal setting, and brand building made easy

Get access now and;

1: Identify your Purpose
2: Build a comprehensive Buyer Persona
3: Find a meaningful 'point-of-difference'
4: Create your Brand Pillars
5: Create your Brand Promise
6: Create an actionable Vision Statement
7: Develop your own Brand Personality
8: Create a strategic 1 year, and 5 year brand plan

Special Offer

I

Adv   month-to-month

You s____ a further 40% by paying annually!

Pick a package and sign up in less than 60 seconds.
Change or cancel at any time.

This offer has been updated - To get a 10% discount off the retail price of Plan2Brand use the promotional code **d2d10off** when paying in full, or **d2d10offinstalment** when paying in instalments.
Visit www.plan2brand.com to redeem this offer

Take off now! Jump onto: **www.plan2brand.com**
Use the exclusive promo code 'P2B' on checkout

Contents

In defense of the book   1
Foreword by Jack Delosa   3
How to use this book   5
Introduction   9

Part 1   17
  What is branding?   18
  A brand new reality   28
  Lessons from the leaders   35
  Start with plan   43
  Introducing the seven steps   48

Part 2: The 7 steps to differentiating and dominating   55
  Step 1: Bring your purpose to life   57
          A word about research   76
  Step 2: Identify your ideal customer   81
  Step 3: Position yourself for success   101
  Step 4: Build the foundations that guide your brand   121
  Step 5: Create your promise   129
  Step 6: Clarify your vision   139
  Step 7: Show them you're human   149

Your Brand Foundations   165

A final thought   169

Your quick-start guide: 22 ways to differentiate   171

About The Author   177

In defense of the book

What is a book? A teacher, a landscape, a window? Marcel Proust wrote that authors may call their books conclusions, but for the reader they are called provocations. That's what I want this book to be, a provocation. Yes there are some answers, but more than that, I want you to ask yourself questions. I want to challenge your comfort zone. I want to encourage you to see possibilities for your business, to understand that it's not just a business, it's a strategic platform, and I want you to discover a new felt passion for your business.

Foreword

**Jack Delosa, founder of The Entourage and
BRW Young Rich List Member**

The business world has changed. Significantly. How we start and build businesses has changed, but more important, we as consumers have changed. Although the business world is still addicted to professionalism at all costs, we live in an era where consumers want so much more than 'professional'. Today they want purpose.

Today, people crave real. We want brands and people who drop the mask, put aside the suit of professionalism and drop the jargon. We recognise that nobody's perfect and love it when a business has the heart to admit it. In brands we look for a stance that is bold enough to proclaim, "this is who we are and this is who we love to work with." Nothing is more attractive than the business or the person that knows them self and is happy to own their unique DNA.

What makes us different, makes us brilliant. Rather than allowing the need for professionalism to come between human connections, great brands are unapologetically real, finding their true essence, their true purpose and amplifying it to touch the hearts and minds of their audience.

Historically this has been an art. Some brands have a certain magic innate in their DNA and are able to maintain it as the organisation grows. However, most don't. In 'Differentiate to Dominate', Peter outlines how finding magic, and bottling it, is a process that anyone can achieve by forcing us to take a consumer focused approach to how we build businesses.

In my first interaction with Peter was a phone call from Sydney to Melbourne as I was scouring the country to find a branding agency that 'got it'. I knew within minutes that this was a guy who understands consumers, the science behind what builds great brands, and can systematically help people find their purpose and bring it to the forefront of their business through the medium we call 'brand'.

Your brand is not your logo nor is it the colors on your website. Your brand is the heartbeat of your business. It is the feelings your audience associates with you and your business. In 'Differentiate to Dominate' you are about to go on an adventure into the hearts and minds of your consumer and through the science of great business, in a way that will enable you to build something that matters, in a world that is waiting for you to be unapologetically you.

How to use this book

I recently asked 20 business owners and entrepreneurs why they started working for themselves? More than half said one of two things - to be their own boss.

If you're wondering about the second most common dream, I'll get to that soon. Firstly, I need to address one of the greatest challenges every business owner and entrepreneur faces – lack of time!

Between the daily work, the new ideas, new opportunities, the changing technology and our social and private lives, many of us, no, all of us I'm sure, feel like there really aren't enough hours in the day.

In the past 10 plus years the Internet has been the killer. It's like a double-edged sword, a treasure trove of information, yet a rabbit hole of distractions. With reams of facts, figures and opinions flooding our lives, we are all becoming experts at filtering out what we don't need. Running my own firm, I have to be choosey when it comes to what I read, and that goes for books as well.

Yet some books have inspired, educated and changed my life permanently. If you're a small to medium enterprise (SME), and you're passionate about what you do, I believe that 'Differentiate to Dominate' is a resource that deserves your time.

When you discover a completely different way of thinking about your business, huge positive shifts will happen. When you understand how you can transform your business by thinking like the world's greatest brands do, you'll realise that the chapters in this book will give you more of the second thing all entrepreneurs want – control of their lives.

I say this because the seven-step process revealed in the following pages, has changed the way hundreds of businesses owners understand the power of 'thinking like a brand'; transforming their daily routine into a more focused and energetic mission to build an exceptional brand. More importantly, by the time you finish *'Differentiate to Dominate'* you will be able to apply what you've learned immediately.

So before you begin reading, I want to explain how the book works so you get the most out of it. I have broken the book down into two parts.

Part One of the book is an overview of branding: where and why branding as a concept began; how branding evolved; how branding effects all start-up businesses no matter where they are in the world; what's the difference between a business and a brand; what things you need to understand to get the most out of creating a brand.

My aim is to help you in three ways:

1. Provide a context for *'Differentiate to Dominate'.*

2. Help you recognise the importance and opportunities that thinking like a brand offers.

3. Inspire you to be the best you can be, because building a brand is a journey, not a destination.

The third point is really important. Plenty of businesses end in failure. Often not catastrophic failure, they just go off the boil, relying on systems instead of innovating. Innovation comes from inspiration, and by showing you how to build a meaningful brand I hope to help you create businesses that produce change, and in the process make life easier, richer and better for you.

Part Two of the book is the 'how to'. It walks you through my seven-step process, giving you the steps and tools so you can build a set of strong brand foundations for your business. This is because while writers, marketers and designers may get involved with your marketing and promotions when you go out to promote your brand, initially defining the kernel that embodies your brand is your responsibility.

The desired outcome of my process is to:

1. Help you apply strategic thinking to the way you'll build your brand.

2. During that process encourage you to consider what tweaks or changes you could introduce to your business that will help differentiate your service or product.

Because only by standing apart can you stand out!

The best way to describe the outcome of the seven-step process is for you to think of it as a roadmap. Because of the nature of the subject matter, I have designed the process to be interactive. Yes, the concepts taught in the steps are timeless, but the way they get applied to business is changing as you read.

 'Differentiate to Dominate' will teach you the formula, but to give you the most up-to-date application of the seven concept, you will find this 'unlock the worksheet' symbol throughout the book.

This leads you to secret bonus sections on my website. This exclusive content is available free to you as a reader and has been created to give you access to more in-depth worksheets, important updates, videos and bonus offers.

Understanding and embracing strategic branding as a business tool is something every SME needs to do. It's the reason great brands become great, and there's no reason why every business owner can't follow in their footsteps. After all, every great company was small once.

By working through the concepts in each step, and implementing them into your business, it will help you identify a meaningful and differentiated position in your market that you can hold over time. Think of it as the straightest line between two points, the path of least resistance, with the lowest possible risk and the highest return.

Some of the steps may look familiar, and they should. The elements of a strategic plan are not new.

What is new is the way our strategic brand plan fits together. Like a jigsaw, each piece is more valuable when combined with the whole. When completed, your brand foundations guide as many internal business choices as external ones.

While some may find this process challenging, the upside is potentially huge. For SMEs, strategic planning is one of the most misunderstood concepts in business today. By educating yourself about this process you will be ahead of 99% of your competitors, because they don't have a strategic plan!

Entrepreneur Guy Kawasaki said, "The best reason to start an organization is to make meaning – to create a product or service to make the world a better place."

That's what I want to see you do after reading this book.

Introduction

Let's start with a simple question…what do you think when you hear the word 'brand'?

You probably think of a company like Starbucks, whose ubiquitous coffee has become a cultural phenomenon. You might think of Amazon, whose name has become synonymous with books all over the world. You might reflect how Virgin's distinctive logo has infiltrated over 400 different industries. And then there's Nike, the world's most famous sporting company. You might think of Apple, and look at the multitude of i-devices that are likely to be littered around your home. You'll wonder why Coke has a pull much stronger than any generic cola. You'll think about Chanel, and truly believe that it's a better perfume.

And then you might be jealous, because in the hard times we are currently experiencing, these iconic monoliths still manage to increase their profits year after year, cleverly working their way into our global consciousness. We know that the world's greatest brands were almost immune to the last two global recessions. This was not the case for millions of small and medium-sized businesses, many of whom have scaled back or gone out of business altogether over the last ten agonising years.

The secret of domination

You probably think that the brands that achieve the dizzying heights of the Amazons of the world do so because they're sitting on epic piles of money, but you'd be wrong. The reasons for their success are not nearly so crude. The reasons are, in fact, deeply rooted in human nature. Human beings are innately social creatures. We are made to interact and inter-relate. We are either drawn to or uninterested in new relationships for a multitude of reasons we barely understand. Yet over time we surround ourselves with those we feel most comfortable with, and some we stay with forever.

Brand loyalty hinges on this human dynamic, the innate need to belong and be with people we relate to and who share our views and outlook. At a more shallow level, we have a relationship with the brands we trust and embrace because they display characteristics or values we relate to. Building on that sense of belonging between your customer and your brand determines the extent to which you will grow and have brand value.

But how do dominant brands encourage consumers to choose them in the first place? At the end of the day, every product or service must face the judgment of the customer. All they really want to know is how are you different from the competition? How are you better than the competition? What value are you ultimately offering them?

Unfortunately, however, business owners often find it very difficult to articulate the main problem they solve, the need they fill and the unique qualities that differentiate them from their competitors. When asked why we exist, most of us default to describing the industries we are in or the products we make. But if we as business owners aren't clear about why we're in business and what is so special about our product or service, then how confused must our employees and prospects be?

No matter what market you do business in, for your brand to succeed you must achieve differentiation. It's the starting point to every great brand. After all, if your product or service is not different, what are you? You can only be similar, and consumers will assess your product or service on price alone. The truth is the majority of firms in any competitive market are undifferentiated, selling the same homogenous goods as the next guy. This means one thing; you must all sell at whatever price the market determines, which is not a good place to be. You haven't even opened your front door, and you're already destined to become a commodity.

So how do you achieve differentiation? The reason these multinationals have been around for decades now and have managed to weave their way into our daily lives is through a series of concentrated and consistent branding tactics and campaigns.

The truth is they have a plan, a secret weapon, and it's called a brand strategy.

Now, you might think that a brand strategy is the realm of big corporates, that it involves outrageous costs for little return. You might say, "Nah, too hard, all that marketing stuff!" You might wonder how those lucky companies do it, then decide to leave it, cross your fingers and hope your business grows.

Well, I've got good news. You don't have to be a big bloated corporate to be a successful brand. You don't have to have an endless money pit or a wealthy in-law. It's not as challenging as you think and luck has nothing to do with it. It's not about crossing your fingers; it's about steering your own ship.

Unfortunately, most small businesses completely miss this piece of the puzzle.

At college some thirty plus years ago I studied 'communications', which was essentially a graphic communications curriculum, and I graduated as a graphic designer. It was 1986 when I started my design studio, and if an organisation didn't have the budget to work with a full-blown advertising agency, we were the next button on their speed dial. In close to thirty years I have helped literally thousands of small and medium-sized businesses with their branding and marketing efforts.

Looking back, what amazed me so much was that in my first twenty years of business, the term 'strategy' barely ever entered any client conversation. Instead, the conversation always centered on more tangible things like the image, or increasing the size of the logo, or the colours we used, which were all meaningful points in the client's mind, but I now know that back then we were all missing the point.

After thirty years in the business I now know what a brand strategy is, why it matters, and how to execute it. But without a lie, most businesses I deal with still don't think their company needs a strategy. I've spent the better part of my life working with firms who don't give strategy a fleeting thought. Repeatedly I see them struggle to grasp the importance of strategy or truly understand branding, often moving from one design supplier to another and blaming them for their lack of growth.

The concept of strategy as it relates to your business is quite simple: your strategy is intended to inform your marketplace how you compete. Your brand strategy is the key to achieving a differentiated brand. A great business strategy helps you create products services and a great work culture. Every business needs a strategy to minimize risks.

Brands and small business

I love great brands. They make my life easier. In my frantic day-to-day, they help me to quickly narrow my choices, purchase more confidently and get on with my day. This is probably true for you, too. We grow to know the brands we embrace, gaining a clear idea of what we're getting when we interact with them. It's a lot like touching base with a friend, one who gives us a sense of familiarity and stability. The relationship between a customer and a brand is the same as the relationship between true friends – you can count on them.

But while brands make my life easier, there's another reason I love branding - it's the sheer, untapped potential it can bring to entrepreneurs and growing businesses.

Now, just for a moment, think about it:

- Can your business touch and influence your customers the way great brands do?

- Can the average dry cleaner, business coach, or events company think, look, and present like great brands do?

- Can you or the local gym inspire and engage your clientele with your messaging and customer service, to the point where new customers keep coming?

- Can you inform, lead, grow and present a consistent experience at every touch point, increasing profits year on year?

The simple answer is, yes, you can. In fact, if you plan on growing a business in our new speed-of-light, overly optimised world, building a brand is the key to your success.

Now I believe it's time for you, the small business owner and entrepreneur, to do the same by building your own secret weapon – your very own brand strategy. While many of you already have the ingredients and passion, you're probably not thinking like the great brands do. You're not starting with a plan and then implementing it.

While it might at first appear hard for most generic products or services to differentiate, it is possible by connecting at a more emotional level with your prospects and customers through values that matter to them. These values can be rational or emotional, but the degree to which you possess them, and the meaning they have to the consumers (beyond the actual product itself) will determine whether or not consumers perceive your brand as truly differentiated.

Finding that reason to matter rests with you, the business owner. Through *'Differentiate to Dominate'* I will share with you what I have learned in the hope that you will gain a better understanding of what strategy is, why it matters, and what you must do to embrace it and dominate.

In this book I will discuss branding, its background and what dominant brands have in common, then take you through a seven-step process that will help you to position your business as the best choice in the eyes of your prospects. These seven steps will help you differentiate and define your brand foundations. To gain a competitive edge today, the best brands don't just use marketing, messages and symbols to grow. Instead, they strategically manage their brands according to a set of guiding principles that drive business decisions that help them to grow.

The exercises, tools and steps recommended in the second half of this book are based on my thirty years of working with hundreds of small and medium-sized businesses. The thoughts, principles and exercises are by no means a marketing or business plan, but represent the infrastructure that smaller companies fail to build.

By understanding and applying the seven foundational principles of branding, you will be able to find a unique position within your market and create the messaging that will give you more influence, longevity, a better reputation and more connectedness.

My goal is not to lecture you on 'brand strategy' but to inspire and motivate you to come out from under the shadows of your larger competitors and dominate by thinking strategically.

Part 1

What is branding?

'Twenty years from now you will be more disappointed by the things you didn't do than by the ones you did do. So throw off the bowlines. Sail away from the safe harbor. Catch the trade winds in your sails. Explore. Dream. Discover.' –
Mark Twain

What is branding?

While we are all familiar with the word 'brand', it's impossible to find one clear definition the world can agree on. In the infamous words of US Supreme Court Justice Potter Stewart, "I'll know it when I see it." The components of a brand include intangible concepts, confusing marketing theories and double speak that makes little sense but often sounds expensive. Adding to the confusion is the fact that the commercial environment that branding lives within is in a state of constant change, making any definition superfluous over time.

If you Google the word 'brand' you will be faced with hundreds of thousands of websites that have weighed in on the subject and you'll find hundreds of different definitions.

Three of my favorites are:

"A brand is a reason to choose."
– *Cheryl Burgess, Blue Focus Marketing*

"A brand is a promise wrapped in an experience – a consistent promise wrapped in a consistent experience."
– *Charlie Hughes and William Jeanes*

"A brand is a person's gut feeling about a product, service or company."
– *Marty Neumeier*

What we *can* agree on, however, is that your brand is not your logo, or your advertising, website, images, personality, trademark, or your company's look and feel. These are merely expressions or manifestations of your brand.

The best way to truly understand branding is to understand its evolution, from its origin through to the modern concepts.

The evolution of branding

The term 'brand' can first be found in ancient Norway where the Vikings used the word 'brand' as a way of identifying ownership of their animals. Over the coming centuries, branding became established as a form of quasi-legal protection, commonly being used by artisans who marked or branded their work and goods.

It was an English artisan by the name of Josiah Wedgewood who was credited by economists for creating the first modern brand. Wedgewood was born into a family of potters during the industrial revolution and he worked passionately to improve the quality of the crockery of his day. The quality of his goods created so much demand that he was able to charge a premium price and the name 'Wedgewood' soon became synonymous with 'quality'. A brand was born.

Among historians, it's commonly agreed that the pioneering American spirit played the next major role in developing branding into the highly commercial and complex art form we know today.

The rapid expansion of the United States of America was fuelled by a huge railroad network, which not only connected hundreds of new cities but also created efficient new distribution channels on a scale never before seen. Product catalogues carrying the first advertising messages from growing brands were suddenly available nationwide. Newspapers and magazines funded their own growth by carrying the manufacturers' advertisements. The design and advertising industry matured through the increased competitive need for better packaging and marketing materials.

Branding during this early modern era was a relatively simple idea, whereby product manufacturers and their advertising agencies focused on fundamentals such as name, packaging design and perhaps a descriptive positioning statement such as Persil's 'Gives the whites wash' and Victor's 'The big name in motor mowing'.

It was in 1924 when Alfred P. Sloan, General Motors' newly named president, started thinking strategically and began developing different automobile models based on different customer demographics. New cars were produced with the price and quality of each car appealing to what the different consumers they identified could afford.

This shift in marketing thinking didn't go unnoticed and on 13 May 1931, Neil McElroy, President of the American multinational consumer goods company Procter & Gamble (P & G), proposed the modern concept of 'branding'. In a calculated effort to differentiate the increasing number of products P & G promoted, Neil penned an internal memo outlining a new business strategy called 'brand management.' He created the notion that product specialisation and differentiation, instead of business function, would play an important role in the company's future. McElroy's brand management idea ultimately became the foundation of the company's business strategy.

McElroy was frustrated with having to compete not only with soaps from Lever and Palmolive, but also with Ivory, P&G's own flagship product. In his now-famous memo, he argued that more concentrated attention should be paid to Camay, and by extension to other P&G brands as well. In addition to having a person in charge of each brand, he argued there should be a substantial team of people devoted to thinking about every aspect of marketing it. This dedicated group should attend to one brand and it alone. The new unit should include a brand assistant, several 'check-up people', and others with very specific tasks.

The concern of these managers would be one brand only, which would be marketed as if it were a separate business. In this way the qualities of every brand would be distinguished from those of every other. In ad campaigns Camay and Ivory, both P & G products, would be targeted to different consumer markets and therefore would become less competitive with each other. Over the years, 'product differentiation', as businesspeople came to call it, would develop into a key element of marketing.

McElroy's memo ran to a terse three pages, in violation of then President Deupree's model of the 'one-page memo', a P&G custom that had become well known in management circles. But the content of the memo made good sense, and its proposals were approved up the corporate hierarchy and endorsed with enthusiasm by Deupree.

Thus was born the modern system of brand management. It was widely emulated, and in one form or another was followed in the early twenty-first century by many consumer-products companies throughout the world.

Fast-forward a decade and the first truly successful advertising agency was launched in America and named after its founder. Ted Bates & Company grew to become the world's fourth largest agency group and, under Ted's guidance, expanded for twenty-six years without losing a single client.

Ted Bates' creative partner was advertising maverick Rosser Reeves, an advertising pioneer who crafted one of the most popular brand slogans of all time (M&Ms "melt in your mouth, not in your hand").

Ted and Rosser are in many ways the original 'ad men'. It is widely accepted that the popular TV drama 'Mad Men' is based, at least in part, on them.

Ted conducted extensive research during his company's formative years to reverse engineer the success of his clients' companies in order to identify a pattern that could be replicated. His team researched the components of successful advertising campaigns and found that the most successful brands, those that both led their category and produced the highest return on investment (ROI), used what they termed the Unique Selling Proposition or USP. In 1962 Ted Bates & Company's Chairman, Rosser Reeves, penned *'Reality in Advertising'*, in which he shared the concept of the USP and outlined its three pillars:

1. The proposition must be clearly stated to the consumer: 'Buy this product, and you will get this specific benefit.'

2. The proposition itself must be unique. It must express a specific benefit that competitors do not, will not, or cannot offer.

3. The proposition must be strong enough to pull new customers to the product.

The concept of branding in business began to go mainstream in the late 60s and early 70s as the broader concepts of brand image and brand values were developed. In 1972 Al Ries (with Jack Trout) wrote a three-part series of articles on 'positioning' for *Advertising Age* magazine.

Al argued that the consumers' perception of a given brand was more important than product superiority and was instrumental to success. He talked about a brand being all about perceptions, and so, in order to gain a positive reputation and be perceived well by consumers, brands needed to be well positioned in the mind of your customer.

Dubbed 'brand positioning,' this concept remains the standard for developing successful brands to this day.

Ries and Trout explain that while positioning begins with a product, the concept really is about positioning that product in the mind of the customer. This approach is needed because consumers are bombarded with a continuous, almost mind numbing stream of advertising.

In the battle of the car hire brands we can see how Avis tried unsuccessfully for years to win customers, pretending that the market leader, Hertz, did not exist. Finally, Avis began using the line:

"Avis in only No. 2 in rent-a-cars, so why go with us? We try harder."

After launching the campaign, Avis quickly became profitable. Whether Avis actually *tried harder* was not particularly relevant to their success. Rather, consumers finally were able to relate Avis to Hertz, which was number one in their minds.

Through the second half of the twentieth century, western economies experienced phenomenal growth. With the advent of radio and television, the world bore witness to a change that made everybody and every business rethink the way they communicate. Radio has been with us for over a hundred years, and television a little over fifty years. These two technologies have dominated the media and advertising landscape for generations and are still part of the communications fabric that binds our society together. Television and radio took center stage alongside the continued growth of a newly segmented magazine and newspaper industry. The advertising industry continued to grow and increasingly focused on visual concepts and audience segmentation tactics (targeting messages to specific groups) to communicate with the growing number of niche markets like 'stay at home mums' or 'car enthusiasts'.

As international air travel became more affordable and began to shrink our world, branding continued to evolve and slowly took on a more complex, nuanced meaning to a larger, more diverse group of businesses. The once powerful advertising agencies found new competition from public relations agencies, marketing companies and design studios that all spoke about branding from their own perspectives. A graphic designer saw branding from a visual aspect while public relations were normally more interested in one feature of the brand they were seeking publicity for.

It was around the 1970's and 1980's when advertising agencies and other creative groups grew through specialisation, leaving behind the Mad Men era of only servicing national brands and becoming a crucial resource to the growing number of medium-sized businesses.

About thirty years later newspaper and magazine readership peaked and, driven by technology, television and visual entertainment dominated into the turn of the century.

Which brings us to the twenty-first century.

Today we are witnessing another revolution and, as usual, we're having a hard time giving a name to the technology. It has been called the Internet revolution, the social revolution, and now the content revolution. Whatever moniker sticks, one thing is certain; we have only witnessed its birth! And I believe it's the single biggest factor affecting the evolution of branding today.

The media revolution we are currently experiencing is as profound and life-changing as the invention of the printing press in the fifteenth century, which made mass communication possible for the first time. It's as important as Alexander Graham Bell's invention of the telephone, which made voice-based conversation possible. It's as influential as the invention of recorded media – first photos, then recorded sound and eventually movies – which profoundly changed the communications landscape.

The reason this revolution will be as revolutionary as any we have witnessed in the past, is that for the first time in history a platform now exists where two-way communications to many people at the same time is possible. The Internet has disrupted traditional marketing and branding by throwing 'real-time' and 'instant' into the equation as information and messaging are now distributed and shared at a mind-blowing speed. No longer can businesses broadcast their message and call it a day. Consumers are delighting in finally having a voice, in having the power to unsubscribe, to tweet about bad service and to leave bad reviews on rating sites.

In the next chapter we will look at how the media revolution is creating a brave new world of branding. But before we do that, we still need to come up with a definition of branding.

So what is a brand and why is it so important?

Your brand is the entire experience your prospects and customers have when dealing with your company. It's what you stand for, a promise you make and the personality you convey, not just the creative elements that convey your brand. In reality, your brand lives in every day-to-day interaction you have with your market, and should consistently and repeatedly tell your prospects and customers why they should buy from you.

There is a big difference between a business and a brand, so let's look at what exactly separates them:

- Is it the number of locations?

- Is it revenue?

- Is it something you can measure in hashtags and retweets?

What does one have to do before one can legitimately say, "We're not just a business anymore. We're a brand."

There are many elements that combine to make up a brand:

On Wikipedia, a brand is defined as "the name, term, symbol or any other feature that identifies one seller's product distinct from those of other sellers."

This is a good start, to create a brand, one thing you need to be is different from others.

Many brand experts say a brand is "whatever your prospect thinks of when he or she hears your brand name."

In other words, a brand needs a good reputation.

Now think about Virgin's, Apple's or even Aesop's reputation. These brands are successful because they have consistently delivered the highest quality products in their respective markets.

So quality is a big part of building a brand too.

So we're getting closer, but while differentiation, reputation and quality are important foundations for building a brand, they're still just functional characteristics.

Which brings us back to the original question – what is the essence that separates a business from a brand?

Many experts agree that a business becomes a brand when it transcends its category of origin. That is, when it takes an existing core equity, or a particular philosophy, and it infuses that idea into everything it does, furthering its reputation or world view one product, service or line extension at a time.

Lego has transcended its original category – to become one of the most iconic brands in the world today, with line extensions everywhere you look, from video games, robotics, amusement parks to their own feature length films.

Successful branding is all about understanding who you are and being true to what you say you are. It's the sum total of many parts, including your logo, your slogan, the images you convey, the messages you deliver on your website and in your sales materials, the way your employees interact with customers, a customer's opinion of you versus your competition and much more.

The nature of branding has changed radically since Josiah Wedgewood first stamped a plate, and it is no longer a static element. Branding has become a process. And a process that is flexible and malleable, that is not bogged down in fixed ideas but is future-proofed and forward-looking, and exactly what you need to establish and grow a business in the new information rich online world.

A brand new reality

"Products are made in the factory, but brands are created in the mind." – Walter Landor, designer of the Coca-Cola script

You may have often heard it said that there are only two certainties in life, death and taxes. Thanks to the online revolution we can now add 'increased choice for consumers' and, as a result of that increased choice, 'increased competition for businesses'.

The choice pandemic

When I was a young child, a distant family member visited us from Estonia and though I don't remember everything about her visit, one thing has stuck with me all these years. As we were showing her the local shops, we passed a monstrous hardware store that had an immense array of products displayed in the window. Our visitor, who lived under Soviet rule, assumed that as wealthy westerners we owned every type of item she could see in that window. Now while that seemed a little bizarre at the time, it's become closer to the truth than we care to admit.

I was lucky to grow up in a society where personal choices were allowed and encouraged, but when I was growing up the number of choices an individual had was still fairly limited. Back when my parents bought their first car they could choose from a Ford, Holden or a second-hand Vauxhall. Today, however, it's a very different story. At last count, today there are over 300 different vehicles on the market.

In Al Ries and Jack Trout's book *'The 22 Immutable Laws of Marketing'*, the authors identified the 'law of division' to explain the current explosion of choice. They view the market as an ever-dividing sea of categories, not unlike an amoeba dividing in a petri dish.

A business category always starts with a single choice or entity. Automobiles are a great example. The motor car was invented in Europe (Germany, to be specific), and at the start of the 20th Century, all motor vehicles were built one-by-one using the 'coach-building' method.

But in 1908, Henry Ford transformed the car manufacturing industry. He started with the premise that for more people to be able to afford cars, cars needed to be cheaper. This idea sounds simple enough, but in reality, it meant bringing the cost of a car down from around $4000 (twice the average annual income at the time) to less than $1000.

To achieve this Henry introduced the 'assembly line' for motor vehicle construction. By claiming that Model T could be bought in "Any color … so long as it is black", the Ford Motor Company was able to grow sales from 10,000 cars manufactured in 1908 to 472,350 cars in 1915 to 933,720 cars in 1920.

Gradually, however, the market began to expand. Along came Chevrolet, Chrysler and Plymouth in the early 1950s, and eventually the European and Japanese car manufacturers sprang into the market. Two-door cars, SUVs, station wagons, sports cars, high-performance cars and four-wheel drives are now options, and now China is adding to our choices.

The same effect can be seen in the computer industry. The first personal computer manufacturer was 'the big blue' – IBM in partnership with Packard Bell. Fast-forward a few years and not only do we have dozens of computer brands, we have a confusing range of desktops, laptops, tablets, watches and wearables.

If you walk into a supermarket or a huge big-box superstore today, the myriad of choices assault the senses. For those of us running a business it's important to note that this explosion of choice has proliferated into nearly every market segment and will continue to do so.

When it comes to selling your product or service, your prospects and customers are now overwhelmed by choices that seem similar to what you are offering, and I'll bet they struggle to see any significant difference between you and your competitors. If you're not helping them to understand the benefits of buying from *you*, they will invariably buy the least expensive option. Do you really want to go there?

To succeed in these changing times you have two choices: Drop your prices (again), take a stab at some marketing and hope you're noticed first, or understand that your business is more than a business – it's a strategic platform that can be used to leverage your purpose and the key values and attributes that differentiate you. In turn this will build company culture, improve the value you deliver to the customer and set you up for long-term growth.

For over twenty years, we've witnessed our lifestyles change as advances in technology accelerate. Our computers are indispensable, and Alexander Graham Bell wouldn't recognise today's phones if one rang in his hand. Trying clothes on in the shop is becoming passé as we order clothes, flowers, wedding rings, funerals and even our next relationship online. We now get our news, rumors and fake news at the speed of light via fibre optics.

In this breakneck, got-to-get-it-done-yesterday world, people are looking for ways of doing more in less time. To claw back some valuable time, we create shortcuts by using more technology. Instead of diligent research, we simply Google. We invent more technology to fast-forward or skip the ad breaks. We use abbreviations (lol, brb) to make texting faster. The current explosion of technology has not only created more choice, it has in part been responsible for fuelling a choice pandemic. It's because consumers have so much choice that they are turning to technology to make decision-making easier.

Author James Glieck, in his 1999 book 'Faster,' explains why we will continue to see an acceleration of just about everything. Consider the following extract:

'This proliferation of choice represents yet another positive feedback loop--a whole menagerie of such loops. The more information glut bears down on you; the more Internet 'portals' and search engines and infobots arise to help by pouring information your way. The more telephone lines you have, the more you need. The more patents, the more patent lawyers and patent search services. The more cookbooks you buy or browse, the more you feel the need to serve your guests something new; the more cookbooks you need. The complications beget choice; the choices inspire technology; the technologies create complication. Without the distribution and manufacturing efficiencies of the modern age, without toll-free numbers and express delivery and bar codes and scanners and, above all, computers, the choices would not be multiplying like this.'

Today we look to brands to help us cut through the noise and make swifter, better-informed choices. Urban Spoon helps us decide where and what to eat and Catch-of-the-Day helps us choose the cheapest jacket. Using an app we can find the best coffee, the best productivity tips, the best way to exercise, the best way to fall asleep and the right time to wake up. If all else fails, we can reach for our phones to find a doctor.

The battle to stand out

But just as branding becomes more important than ever, and consumers rely on it more than ever, the media revolution is making it increasingly difficult for a brand to stand out from the crowd.

This tyranny of technology means that brands must now compete for space not just on shelves, but on websites and in people's minds. The fight for a brand's presence has become an ugly fight; our eyeballs and minds are the new battlegrounds. The consumer is being hit from every angle. Even the space left in our email and on our desktops is contested. When we look back, there was a time when a few newspapers, TV stations, and radio stations handled all the commercials. But today the traditional thirty-second advertisement is an endangered species. We live in a sound-bite society where the ability to capture a message succinctly and touch people's hearts is the Holy Grail.

Why your business or brand matters and how you compete is more important now than at any other point in history. Consumers today are less influenced by one way marketing messages. They are adept using their DVR to fast-forward through TV commercials and blocking obtrusive online advertising. They are doing more research on the products they intend to buy and are turning to review sites and their friends on social media to vet potential suppliers. As a result, traditional businesses are facing tough questions while coming to terms with their outdated business models.

Today is a pivotal moment in history where we are staring down the barrel of a time-starved world and a younger generation who think and act very differently from the consumers of previous generations. Brand marketing that pulled on emotional heart strings based on a dated value system will have a shrinking role to fill in a world where choice is multiplying and on-demand information is the norm, and our time and resources continue to shrink.

New brands will have increasing difficulty gaining traction if they approach things in the ways of the past. For the established brands, consumer awareness is working well...for now. Their customers have invested time building a relationship with their brand, and there is already a level of comfort and recognition. But...

The times, they are a changin'...

If you want to predict the financial health of any western economy, look no further than the plethora of advertising and marketing companies that service the small and medium-sized business sector.

These creative suppliers are like the proverbial 'canary in the coal mine'. They are the first to see budget cuts when revenue slows down, well before governments admit to it, and the first to see budget increases when the markets start to turn.

I mention this because I have been one of those providers for over thirty years. As I'm witnessing the world slowly drag itself out of arguably the worst recession for many generations, there is one theme I'm repeatedly seeing that distinguishes this economic turnaround from previous ones.

In the past, to be successful in business, firms mostly relied on the control of a scare resource. It could be a battle for marginal lands, the race to build a newspaper monopoly or, at its ugliest, the cutthroat tactics involved with trading stocks. Often described as the 'zero-sum game,' it's defined as a situation in which a win by one person means a loss to the other, and that's how business was done! You owned the house; somebody paid you to rent it.

Well the times they are a changin'. The tactics that matter today and make a difference are less about the battle for control, and increasingly about innovation, new ideas, better service and disruption and the importance of influence.

If you're struggling with today's ever-changing business environment, you're not alone. Every business I consult with faces the same challenges. The transition from traditional push marketing to what many are now calling 'pull media' has left many business leaders scratching their heads in confusion. But while many businesses and advertisers are still reeling from the sudden changes, many are adapting and embracing this latest media revolution.

The businesses that are prospering are leveraging change in one way or another. They are remodeling, remaking, and in many cases, reinventing themselves, their products or their processes.

They don't simply start their business; they plan it and look for a better, uncontested position in the marketplace instead of fighting for common ground.

Helping these businesses to get heard, get found, and gain reach are now a plethora of new digital tools that have democratised the creation and distribution of content. Businesses wanting to grow no longer need to use expensive advertising agencies when they plan and follow a strategy that sets them apart from the competition.

Those that are playing a different game, listening to and adapting to the new customer/technology paradigm, are thinking deeply about issues such as their purpose and vision to find new fields to build in, while those who stubbornly hold onto the ways of the past continue to feel the pain.

Today, consumers expect to be treated as brand partners and not as just a transaction. Understanding this new paradigm is the key to delivering the right experience every time.

The seven steps in this book have been designed to help you find the unique qualities that separate you from your competitors, so that you're not seen as another choice, but as the only choice. But before we get to the seven steps, let's have a look at how we can learn from the big boys.

Lessons from the leaders

'Any damn fool can put on a deal, but it takes genius, faith and perseverance to create a brand.' – David Ogilvy

Have you ever stopped to think how Apple, DHL or Virgin became such dominant empires in so little time? Have you considered how the Nikes of the world get each moving part of their business, from their branding and design through to their marketing and PR, so in sync? Their brand, mission and products move with the precision of a fine Swiss watch.

Smaller companies, however, often struggle with integrating branding into their planning process. This is understandable, as most small business owners do not have a marketing degree or practical branding knowledge and experience, and it is this lack of education that often limits business growth. Sure, if you're flush with cash you can bring in a large marketing and PR firm to create and execute a brand strategy based on your vision, but what about the rest of us with smaller budgets? Is there a way for us to create and nurture a brand?

Of course there is. I have spent ten years studying dominant brands to identify what they have in common, and I have discovered that much of what they do has nothing to do with the size of either their company or their budget. The following are differentiators I identified when studying and learning from dominant brands.

1) Dominant brands change people's lives

There are only two ways to approach branding: branding that positions a product as a solution to the customers' wants and needs as they already exist, or branding that steps up and says, 'I want to change people's lives, change perceptions and change the way people spend their day.' If you think about it, almost all great brands changed something.

- Nike has changed the way we think about sport

- Armani the way that we dress

- Google has changed the way we access information

- Apple has changed how we share music and memories

- Uber has changed the way we get around a city

- Air BnB has changed the way we house ourselves in different cities and countries

2) Dominant brands make waves

Brands that make waves, big waves, reap the rewards. TED made waves, Cirque du Soleil made waves, and in their own market Bunnings made waves, all by bringing something new and unique to the table. On the other hand, Masters (a failed competitor to Bunnings) was merely following a trend and paid the price. If you want to start a home improvements organisation, you better be prepared to take large risks in order to create big waves in an already competitive market, because if all you are doing is following it, you're following it down. That's not where you want to be.

3) **Dominant brands take risks**

Running a business or building a brand comes with a certain amount of personal risk. What are you prepared to risk to build your dream brand? Brands that get noticed often break values or traditions. *The Voice* and *The X Factor* have had to cop a lot of criticism from within the music industry to make waves and make their creators very rich.

Where are you prepared to show up and what are you prepared to say? Moving forward and going out to the world with an idea that changes industry norms has many risks, and you're more than likely going against somebody's better judgment, so be prepared for flak from partners, the bank, your community, or even the press.

4) **Dominant brands have an enemy**

How do you rally the troops or find believers and supporters? How do you get people to believe in what you believe in, driving them to help you succeed and grow? What if I suggested taking a leaf out of the politicians' book? Find an enemy and leverage it!

To galvanise support we often see politicians identifying and attacking an enemy – gun laws, street violence, hospital waiting lists. Why? Because it's a great tactic to bring together people who share a common mind; it stirs up feelings of being on the same team and provides a clear focus.

All great brands have an enemy.

Virgin Airlines has its enemy: expensive airline tickets. Their entire business model is based on making travel affordable to the masses.

Apple has an enemy: boring, unnecessarily complex technology.

DHL has an enemy: slow, unreliable delivery services. Their business model is focused on 'when it has to be there every time on time.'

Your enemy will be something your brand fundamentally opposes and wants to change. Depending on what you stand for, it could be an injustice or a belief. It could be an outdated way of working, a system different to yours or simply an assumption.

5) **Dominant brands embrace change**

Adaption has underpinned the evolution of the human race, and it should be no different for business, especially in the face of the online revolution. We are at the beginning of arguably the biggest change the world has experienced since the beginning of the industrial revolution, and change we must.

As the owner of a growing business and someone who is planning to build a brand, ask yourself what is allowed to change? It could be pricing, customer service or the way you deal with the environment. To succeed today, you must understand that branding is everything and that you're in charge of everything, thus everything is potentially up for change, and up to you.

> ### *Take Lego, for example.*
>
> *Many people didn't realise it but in 2004 the fourth-largest toymaker in the world, Lego, was in big trouble. The Lego Group had lost money four out of the seven years from 1998 through 2004 and Group executives estimated that the company was destroying $337,000 in value every day.*
>
> *Looking at Lego now it's hard to comprehend that they were on the brink of bankruptcy. They were turning over US$1.35 billion, there were 62 bricks out there for every person in the*

world, their mini figures were the world's largest population and they were one of the world's largest tire manufacturers!

Lego's senior executives were forced to ask themselves the question, "Why does Lego exist?" and began to rebuild the brand framework, seen below, from the ground up, creating a completely new set of brand foundations to re-focus the company.

Mission: Inspire and develop the builders of tomorrow

Aspiration: Globalize and innovate the LEGO system-in-play

Play Promise: Joy of building, value of creation

Planet Promise: Positive impact

Partner Promise: Mutual value creation

People Promise: Succeed together

Spirit: Only the best is good enough

Pillars: Imagination, creativity, fun, learning, caring, quality

Ultimately it was the combination of smarter management combined with creativity that saved the company. Change had to be embraced or they would have met the same fate as Kodak.

6) **Dominant brands measure their success**

In the past everything was incapable of being measured accurately, except maybe the bottom line. TV, direct mail, radio and sponsorship are totally immeasurable. Media purchases went something like 'We think we should buy this.' Readership, circulation and fuzzy statistics around demographics were merely a guide.

Building a brand now can be a science, thanks to Google, thanks to email and thanks to everything that's being developed online on a daily basis. Almost everything digital is measurable, so from the start you have to ask yourself 'What will I measure?' Some numbers you don't have to care about, but don't be lazy – just because some things are hard to measure, it doesn't mean you shouldn't.

At its most basic level, these are five critical marketing metrics you should measure:

- **Revenue.** Looking at how much revenue each channel is actually generating gives you a more objective way of identifying your most effective channels.

- **Cost per lead.** Rather than using this as a general figure, filter it down to establish the cost per lead for each channel you use and identify which are the most cost effective.

- **Website traffic to lead ratio.** Page views and unique visitor numbers might look good in a report but they can't tell you much. Look to see where visitors are actually coming from – direct, referral or organic – what they're doing when they arrive and how many are being converted into leads and customers.

- **Landing page conversion rates.** This helps you establish whether your content and landing pages are resonating with your personas. You can then tinker with them, changing each bit at a time to see what clicks – is it the wrong offer?

- **Customer lifetime value and churn rate.** Knowing how many customers you have is all well and good, but how much and how often are they buying? And for how long do they remain a customer?

7) **Dominant brands do one thing well**

The best way to survive and prosper is to be better than your competitors at one thing.

When Google management first wrote their company philosophy, '10 things we know to be true', they had only been operating for a few years. The second item on their list of principles designed to guide their entire business is:

'It's best to do one thing really, really well.'

So if it's good enough for Google, I think it's safe to assume it's a tactic you should adopt.

Doing one thing really well and identifying a niche in our cluttered business market is one of the most important considerations when you are thinking about your differentiation. Current-day consumers are bombarded with marketing messages about thousands of products every day.

As a consequence of this onslaught, consumers simply don't see a difference in many competing products and are left to choose using the lowest common denominator, price. By building a solid brand that does one thing well and connects with your consumers on an emotional level, you can bypass price considerations.

The idea of doing one thing well makes a lot of sense. It is in this hyper-busy world where information is at our fingertips that brands that help the consumer by making choices easier will outperform the competition. Consumers are increasingly relying on brands that understand their needs and don't let them down because they provide a clear, unambiguous solution to their problems.

8) Dominant brands are different

No matter what market you do business in, for your brand to succeed you must achieve true differentiation. The most successful products and services are highly differentiated from their competitors.

Look at any shelf in a supermarket. There are plenty of savories to buy, but there is only one Cheezels. There is only one Mars Bar. There is only one Pez (remember them!). You will find a range of Goats Cheese, but there is a product leader. In Australia's case it's Merridth.

Differentiation is the starting point for building every great brand, and lack of perceived value directly relates to a lack of differentiation.

We all know that anybody can be different on the surface. The key is being different in a way that:

- Matters to your target market.

- Creates a competitive advantage.

- Is sustainable in the long term.

So how do you create a differentiated business? With a strategy, of course.

Start with plan

'**Companies that enjoy enduring success have core values and a core purpose that remain fixed while their business strategies and practices endlessly adapt to a changing world.**' – Jerry Porras and Jim Collins

---

So how do dominant brands create and execute their brand strategy? How do they connect with their prospects at a more emotional level?

Firstly, they never begin with design!

Let's face it, it's tempting just to start printing out business cards, pop out a website and start hunting for clients. It's tempting to start trading and getting money into the door, but that's a huge mistake. By jumping in and simply starting your business (sound familiar?), you're missing the first and most important step: crafting your strategy. The imagery, style and colours you choose for your marketing collateral and website may show the world what you look like, but what about the most important aspect of your business: who you are, what you stand for and why should somebody buy from you?

Having worked intimately with both international brands and SME's for over 30 years, I've thought a lot about why smaller businesses often jump in and simply start, while the fortune 500's of the world take a completely different approach.

The one fundamental thing I've discovered that all great brands do to become great, (and virtually immune to worldwide recessions,) that distinguishes them from the average business is:

> Great brands have a **strategy first approach**.
> SME's have a **tactics first approach.**

Once the domain of the world's biggest brands, a strategy first approach has never been more important if you want to build long-term success.

Loosely referred to as 'strategic branding', or creating a 'brand strategy', it's involves a planning process that applies innovation, strategic thinking and operational planning to develop business strategies that have a greater chance for success.

Nobody would build a house without a detailed plan, so surely the same principle applies to businesses?

So what is a brand strategy?

A Brand Strategy answers the question: **"Why should somebody buy form you instead of the competition."**

It is a process of examining everything you do and understanding the needs of your customers and ensuring that all of this is linked to clearly defined strategic imperatives.

A Brand Strategy knits together three disciplines:

1) Strategic Thinking – that's the "What" and the "Why", that is what should we be doing and why.

2) Strategic Positioning – that's the "How" you will compete in the market and differentiate.

3) Operational Planning – the specific goals, objectives and tactics at a high level.

The purpose of a Brand Strategy is to create a roadmap, or a plan, that is a coherent, unifying, integrative framework for decisions. Especially one that influence the direction of the business and its competitive advantage.

Unfortunately, however, when most small-business owners hear the words 'brand,' 'brand strategy' and 'positioning', they think 'big brands.' They shake their heads and lament that they don't have the resources to do big-brand marketing.

Nothing could be further from the truth. It's actually quite the opposite.

If any business should focus on its brand strategy, it's a small business or an entrepreneur. The time and energy you'll invest planning and building a brand is guaranteed to give you a better return on your marketing spend. By having a good brand strategy, you minimise wastage and increase your dollar's effectiveness. Planning and thinking strategically gives clarity around where to spend your money in order to achieve your goals more efficiently and effectively.

For one simple reason: A brand strategy will give you clarity and focus.

Focus is a small-business owner's best friend, and working on your brand strategy and your positioning will bring you greater focus than ever before. It forces multiple decisions on what will best build your brand.

As you work through the following steps and formulate your brand strategy, your answers to the questions I pose will guide much of your future decision-making and make that process almost immediate. A good strategy will give you the clarity you need to move your business forward.

When you approach your branding strategically, everyone in your business, through to your customers and prospects, will all be driven and influenced by your purpose, values and beliefs. This is the real engine behind your logo and your company sign. By managing a brand properly, building your own DNA into your product, service and people, it automatically gives you a competitive advantage.

A well thought-through strategy provides you with clarity for growth and affects every aspect of your business and should not be underestimated. In the following seven chapters I explain each step you should address and provide links to worksheets you can download to complete each exercise.

The seven steps you are about to discover guide and propel practically every one of the world's most successful brands. From Virgin through to Apple, PayPal and Amazon, to varying degrees, they all plan and build their brands using them.

These steps represent the core foundations that help them to:

- Grow more rapidly

- Attract more loyal customers

- Become the clear choice above their competitors

- Build a website their customers will love

- Create powerful, clear and consistent messages

- Attract and assemble great teams

- Grow through better partnerships

- Get a higher ROI on their marketing investment.

By embracing each step into your business it will help you identify a meaningful and differentiated position in your market that you can hold over time.

Think of it as the straightest line between two points—the path of least resistance, with the lowest possible risk and the highest return.

Some of the steps may look familiar, and they should. The elements of a strategic plan are not new, many have been around for 50+ years.

What is new is the way our strategic brand plan fits together. Like a jigsaw, each piece is more valuable when combined with the whole.

When finished, your brand foundations guide as many internal business choices as external ones.

While some may find this process challenging, the upside is potentially huge. By educating yourself about this process you will be ahead of 99% of your competitors, because, to be frank, they don't have a strategic plan!

Introducing the seven steps

The beauty of the seven essential ingredients to building a brand is that they start, and revolve around, you. As a small business owner you're in a very fortunate position today because great brands, even small ones (no, especially small ones) are more powerful when they are represented by the passion you have for your business. The steps you are about to go through will help you to unlock that passion in ways that are meaningful to your business and your prospects.

The process is designed to help you gain clarity and focus and organize the hundreds of thoughts you have about your service or product to be more relevant and focused on your customer. Humans are social creatures, and online today they are constantly looking for trust before they make a purchase decision. The seven steps will help you to find and highlight, in a way that matters to your prospects, the authenticity that leads to the trust everybody is looking for before spending money with or recommending a brand.

You will also learn how to build a brand that matters, which is supported by credible and meaning evidence, and one that speaks to your prospect's needs and wants. Every step is a step towards clear differentiation in ways that matter to your market.

The steps form a roadmap, a plan of how you will connect with the customer and beat the competition.

That is the how, what, where, when and to whom you plan on communicating and delivering your brand messages.

- Where you advertise is part of your brand strategy.

- Your distribution channels are also part of your brand strategy.

- And what you communicate visually and verbally are part of your brand strategy too.

Today building a website is getting easier. Putting out some Facebook ads is a no-brainer. Sending out an email newsletter can be outsourced to a VA at very little cost.

The challenge is answering the question 'why does your product/service matter and why should someone buy from you, and not the competition?

The process we have created helps you to build your Brand Foundations and answer these exact questions.

When you work through the seven steps and implement the concepts and actions into your business, the combined result is a way of thinking and running your business from a strategic perspective.

These are the steps you should ideally address before creating a name for your business and creating a logo design. Each of the issues raised in the coming chapters are designed to help you solidify all of your business ideas and options into a clearer differentiated brand and business concept. Once you have gone through all of the steps you will be able to create concise statements and messages that will support your differentiation in ways that convince prospects that your product or service is superior to the competition.

The steps are also designed to help you define the value your brand represents to your prospects and how to express that to the marketplace.

It's the business owners who are disciplined enough to stay focused on these higher impact actions who will dominate.

In summary, the seven steps are:

- **Bring your purpose to life** - Identify your WHY, the reason you exist. It's far more important than any business goals you have. A company with purpose and vision will attract talented staff, strategic alliances and customers who come back time and time again. Articulating a purpose broader than making money will guide strategies and actions, open new sources for innovation, and help people express corporate and personal values in their everyday work.

- **Identify your ideal customer and the emotional reasons they should buy from you** - Today it's no longer good enough to just put your product or service out there and hope people will buy from you. To succeed today you must understand your customer's needs and wants, and in your marketing address their pain points, using messaging that connects at a deeper emotional level.

- **Position yourself for success** - The secret sauce that ultimately differentiates great brands from so-so brands is a concept known as positioning, and your brand will have trouble establishing itself without taking a hard look at where you sit in your market in relation to the competition. Ideally you need to find a niche within your market that nobody else services.

- **Build the foundations that guide your brand** - Establishing brand pillars that define the customer experience you want to create, and telling your market through actions not words, will uniquely position your business so everybody who interacts with your brand understands what you stand for and how that benefits them.

- **Create your promise -**Your brand promise is your core selling idea – the shortest and simplest way to demonstrate to your prospects, customers, staff and stakeholders exactly what you deliver and the value that differentiates your product or service. Articulating your brand promise is one of the most powerful things you can do within your business.

- **Clarify your vision -** The reason most businesses don't achieve their goals or desires comes from a direct lack of a clear vision. Building a 'brand' is very different from building a business. It requires a long-term view and a 'vision' that supports your purpose. Think about it – how can anything meaningful happen without a vision?

- **Show them you're human** - Your brand's attributes make up your personality, the set of characteristics that define how you want people to remember your brand. It has long been accepted that customers don't choose products based on their features alone, but also base their selections on symbolic value. When a customer identifies with the personality of a brand this inspires trust, encourages brand loyalty and makes a brand memorable.

Remember – communicating the various aspects of your strategy internally and externally is the key to driving growth. The clarity that comes from having a brand strategy affects every aspect of your business and should not be underestimated.

By working through the seven strategic branding steps your ultimate aim is to either:

> **A) Change some things within your existing business to create a compelling brand based on differentiation.**

or

> **B) If you're creating a new business, develop a strategic plan that gives your new brand a substantial point of difference and longevity.**

Remember, that this relies more on heuristic thinking than algorithmic thinking – meaning that there is no set path or mathematical formula to follow, but you still need rigor and a process to follow otherwise you'll drift from one thought to another. That's why the steps exist.

As you work through each exercise, you will more than likely find yourself needing to go back and revisit earlier steps and review them. That's perfectly OK. Give yourself time to re-read your answers and review them in a fresh light. Some of the questions are very personal, whereas others may require some homework.

Don't rush through each stage and if possible, find a brainstorming buddy to help keep you on track.

The 7 steps in action

To give you an idea about how your Brand Foundations come together, at the end of the following seven steps (apart from step 2), the strategic elements of the Brand Foundations for a fictitious fruit and vegetable store, **Organic Fresh** are gradually revealed. When completed (at the end of Module 7) they work in harmony to create the whole essence of and direction for the brand both on an internal and external level.

Part 2

The seven steps to differentiating and dominating

"Until what you say is more important than what you sell, you don't have a brand."
– Peter Engelhardt

Step 1

Bring your purpose to life

> 'You can't build a great building on a weak foundation. You must have a solid foundation if you're going to have a strong superstructure.'
> – Gordon B. Hinckley

Step 1: Bring your purpose to life

In business terms, your purpose is the *why* your business exists and I believe this is far more important than any business goals you have. Your purpose comes from your strongly held beliefs. It informs the values that guide you and your business, reflects how you want to influence the world, and it's unique to you.

And it's the first vital step towards your brand's differentiation.

To convince today's millennials and grow tribes to propel your brand along, the clearer and more focused you are on your purpose, the easier it will be to build your brand. Having clarity and focus on how you'll communicate your purpose and vision to the world is one of the best ways smaller businesses can differentiate and succeed.

What you believe is everything. When you lead with purpose, integrity follows. This is what everyone is searching for online today – someone to trust. If you think about the brands that have iconic status, like Nike and Apple, or great politicians throughout history for that matter, it's their purpose that resonates so deeply with us.

It's because of what they stand for that they are able to stand apart.

Think about Apple – their advertising strategies start with why *they make computers, not* how *they make them. They focus on selling the lifestyle they know their market aspires to, instead of the all too obvious 'our processors are faster than our competitors'.*

Aēsop on the other hand believe everyone should have access to the highest quality bathroom products. As a company they have long shied away from advertising and "the vulgarities of what retail can embody" and have managed to build a successful brand on rigorous ingredient and product research and attention to detail.

Emma & Tom's are committed to helping all Australians look after themselves by offering nutritious, minimally processed whole fruit products that are good for you, and taste great too! They too have launched into a market dominated by international brands and have had tremendous success through their commitment to quality ingredients.

Dominating the sports apparel industry is Nike who believe "if you have a body, you are an athlete" and they want to inspire every one of us to become the best we can be. That is their purpose and it drives everything they do.

Each of these brands demonstrate how standing for something that resonates with a tribe helps a business to go beyond the functional aspect of their product by tapping into human emotions.

In our connected world, today's savvy consumer is increasingly being influenced by, and buying from, brands they see as relevant and, above all, ones they can trust. To demonstrate what I mean when I say that, during my presentations and workshops I often show Simon Sinek's inspiring TED talk, 'How Great Leaders Inspire Action.' If you are in business and you haven't seen it, as a gift to yourself make sure you do. See link below.

According to Simon Sinek, the fundamental difference between the Apples of the world and everyone else is that they start with why.

What does that even mean? To explain this concept, Sinek has developed what he calls the "Golden Circle," (Figure 1.1) The golden circle has three layers:

Here is a link: http://bit.ly/1a1B6s6

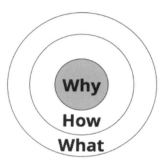

Fig 1.1

- Why - This is the core belief of the business. It's why the business exists.

- How - This is how the business fulfills that core belief.

- What - This is what the company does to fulfill that core belief.

Sounds simple, but what Sinek found is that most companies do their marketing backwards. They start with their 'what' and then move to 'how' they do it. Most of these companies neglect to even mention why they do what they do. More alarmingly, many of them don't even know why they do what they do.

Not Apple. Apple starts with 'why'. It is the core of their marketing and the driving force behind their business operations. To help illustrate this point, imagine if Apple also started backwards by creating a marketing message that started with 'what'. It would sound something like this:

"We make great computers. They're user friendly, beautifully designed, and easy to use. Want to buy one?"

While these facts are true, I'm not sold. Deep down we instead want to know *why* they are great and user friendly. Turns out Apple has figured this out over the years and knows better. Here's what a real marketing message from Apple might actually look like:

"With everything we do, we aim to challenge the status quo. We aim to think differently. Our products are user friendly, beautifully designed, and easy to use. We just happen to make great computers. Want to buy one?"

See how different that feels? Because Apple starts with 'why' when defining their company, they are able to attract customers who share their fundamental beliefs. As Sinek puts it, "People don't buy what you do. They buy why you do it." Starting with 'why' makes Apple more than just a computer company selling features, and that's why their products have flourished while their competitors' products with similar technology and capabilities have often flopped.

Having a purpose, and being true to it not only attracts customers, it also has a positive impact on your business internally. Think about this for a minute: Have you discovered your 'why'? Or are you still working to perfect your 'what'?

The default position for most businesses is simply keeping everybody working hard every day to keep the customer happy, to increase sales, and, wherever possible, keep employees motivated. However, it's not uncommon for business owners at some stage to come to the realisation that something is still missing.

You may have a mission or vision statement, you may have clear reasons why you're in business, but does that reason truly 'fulfill your why'? That is, does it lead you toward where you want to end up in life? If the direction you set is based on a 'what', and not your 'why', then you'll likely struggle when it comes to making hard decisions and find it harder to say no to some opportunities and yes to others, let alone attract the right tribe.

The fact is, most companies don't have a *why*. Many have missions that are platitudes or clichés at best, like "Creating amazing shareholder value" or "To be a fastest growing…." or "Delivering the best product or service…" These statements can only give you a benchmark, at best. They are not purposes and they definitely don't give you or your team a true sense of meaning that makes anyone want to support you.

Why '*why*' matters so much

We spend more time at work than we do with our loved ones and family. As our careers and bank balance grow, and as we age, it's human nature to think more about, and begin seeking, a greater sense of purpose and meaning.

- Why am I doing what I'm doing?

- What impact am I really making?

- What will I leave behind?

- Why does my business, or the business I work for, matter?

Struggling with these questions and thoughts is not unusual. It's rare for most businesses to have a basic value proposition, let alone a purpose steering the ship. At first, imagining a purpose driving your company might feel a little strange or hippy, but there are very sound economic reasons why your business should lead with purpose.

In a famous six-year landmark project at Stanford University, James C. Collins and Jerry I. Porras studied 18 exceptional and enduring companies. Each business was studied in direct comparison to one of their top competitors.

Porras and Collins determined that the primary driver for building a successful company is the ability to nurture a clear purpose.

Amazingly, their research discovered the companies who preserved their purpose and vision and embodied it in their business plan, such as Coca-Cola does, have outperformed their competitors on the stock market by a factor of 12 since 1925.

There's probably no better example of a successful purpose driven brand than Blake Mycoskie's Toms Shoes. Blake found his passion, which became his marketing story, while taking a break from his projects and work and travelling in Argentina. He was 29 years old and running his fourth entrepreneurial startup: an online driver's education program for teens. Blake's main mission was to simply lose himself in Argentina's culture, learning the national dance (the tango), playing the national sport (polo), and, of course, drinking the national wine (Malbec).

Blake quickly got used to wearing the national shoe, the alpargata, a soft, casual canvas shoe worn by almost everyone in the country. He saw this incredibly versatile shoe everywhere, in the cities, on the farms and in the nightclubs.

Later during his travels, he met an American woman in a café who was volunteering on a shoe drive, a new concept to Blake. She explained that many kids lacked shoes, even in relatively well-developed countries like Argentina, where charities often tried to help but struggled constantly with finding funds.

Blake genuinely found this heartbreaking and he decided to spend a few days travelling from village to village, witnessing for himself the intense pockets of poverty just outside the bustling capital. He admits somewhere in the back of his mind he knew that poor children around the world often went barefoot, but now, for the first time, he saw the real effects of being shoeless: the blisters, the sores, the infections.

He wanted to do something about it. But what?

Looking for solutions in the world he already knew, business and entrepreneurship, Blake hit on an idea. Why not create a for-profit business to help provide shoes for these children? Why not come up with a solution that guaranteed a constant flow of shoes, not just whenever kind people were able to make a donation? In other words, maybe the solution was in entrepreneurship, not charity.

The concept was simple. Start a shoe company that makes a new kind of alpargata and for every pair sold, he would give a pair of new shoes to a child in need.

Don't you just love it? Sell a pair of shoes today, give a pair of shoes tomorrow. Blake was so energised by the idea that even without connections in the shoe business, he knew he could make this happen. He decided to call his new business 'TOMS' and eventually settled on the positioning statement "Shoes for a Better Tomorrow." When you ask Blake why he chose the name Tom, and not Blake, he says "It's not about a person. It's about a promise, a better tomorrow."

The lesson is: "Find your story." For Blake, it was the simple idea that for every pair of shoes that Toms Shoes sold, another pair would be given to children in need. As of May 2015, more than 35 million pairs of shoes have been given away, with no end in sight. His purpose is the thing that has been driving his growth and his success.

Tom's Shoes is proof that purpose, that starting with something that matters in mind, is key to growing a differentiated brand because it's the easiest way to attract others to join you in your cause. Why should anyone care if your business succeeds or fails? Unfortunately, for most businesses, the harsh reality is that there really isn't a good reason (outside of your employees wanting to keep their jobs).

What can a purpose do for my business?

Having a purpose helps you to:

- Bring greater focus to many business activities.

- Guide strategies and actions. By associating your brand with a purpose, you're creating a mechanism that will provide clarity and consistency as your company grows. When your business begins to scale, you will find your purpose continually simplifies many day-to-day decisions.

- Create differentiated products and marketing.

- Foster innovation.

- Create a strong, committed team. When you have a purpose, and every member of your team believes what you believe, your plans, ambitions and effort stand a much better chance of hitting the target.

- Empower your staff to make decisions.

- Establish a culture-driven business.

So what does a purpose statement look like?

As we have discovered, your purpose statement articulates why you do what you do, why your organisation exists and why you serve a higher purpose (your cause).

Let's look at a few famous ones:

3M	Our purpose is to solve unsolved problems innovatively.
Merck	Our purpose is to preserve and improve human life.
Walt Disney	Our purpose is to make people happy.
SETI Institute	Our purpose is to explore, understand, and explain the origin, nature, prevalence and distribution of life in the universe.
Hewlett-Packard	Our purpose is to make technical contributions for the advancement and welfare of humanity.
Sony	Our purpose is to experience the joy of advancing and applying technology for the benefit of the public.
Wal-Mart	Our purpose is to give ordinary folk the chance to buy the same things as rich people.

These examples are all from large companies, but the reason for this book is to inspire the SMEs of the world to walk in their footsteps. So let's look at a few examples from brands you might never have heard of. The following are all from SME's, which I think you'll find more relatable.

ILBIJERRI Theatre Islander Company	To create challenging and inspiring theatre by Aboriginal and Torres Strait artists that give voice to our culture.
Pukka Herbs	Through the incredible power of plants we will inspire you to lead a more conscious life. We will strive every day to help create a Pukka Planet benefiting people, plants and planet.
Aesop - Skin, hair	To formulate skin, hair and body care products of the finest quality with a proven and body care record of safety and efficiency.
IAG (Insurance Australia Group)	To help people manage risk and recover from the hardship of unexpected loss.
Car Next Door (Care sharing platform)	To reduce the amount of carbon going into the atmosphere.

Your purpose statement

The adoption of a purpose, and the alignment of your brand strategy with that purpose, is the single most important job that you as a leader has to perform. The challenge you face is there is no simple or standard way to find and express your purpose. Being clear, honest, authentic and genuine about yourself is one of the best starting points I can give you.

Following is one exercise I use in my workshops that has helped dozens of business owners.

Understanding your moral attribute

This exercise asks you to identify which moral attribute you most closely relate to. We know that the most successful organisations, over time, are those in which people act consistently and decisively, innovating and building high-quality relationships. Your task as the leader, no matter how big or small your business, is to stimulate these kinds of actions, reliably and continually. The leaders who can do this are not magicians. Consciously or not, they have learned how to deploy a conceptual tool that allows them to inspire and lead an organisation towards an enduring competitive advantage.

That conceptual tool is called a 'moral attribute'. Think of it as a value that when articulated appeals to an individual's sense of what is right and what is worthwhile.

I designed this exercise using observations made by Nikos Mourkogiannis, one of the world's greatest experts in the field of Strategic Leadership. According to Mourkogiannis, there are four moral attributes on which a successful purpose can be based.

In the following exercise you will discover which moral attribute you most closely relate to. It will be either:

1. Discovery

2. Excellence

3. Altruism

4. Heroism

Let's look at the four moral attributes in more detail.

The moral attribute Discovery centers on the search for the new. Discovery put America on the map, men on the moon and the dot-coms in business. Sony, IBM, Google and many technologically based companies have succeeded by making innovation and exploration the center of their effort.

The moral attribute Excellence focuses on providing the best possible product or service. Excellence built the great cathedrals of Europe and today's most successful professional and creative businesses. Apple, BMW, and Warren Buffett's firm Berkshire Hathaway have all built their identity around the artistry of their endeavors.

The moral attribute Altruism is built on compassion. Altruism is the driving force of any organization that exists primarily to help others, like many political parties or most charities. Nordstrom, Hewlett-Packard, and even Wal-Mart, have established appeal around the idea that they are, first and foremost, making their customers happy.

The moral attribute Heroism sets the standards for everyone else to follow. Heroism resulted in the Roman Empire, Wimbledon champions Serena and Venus Williams and many spectacular growth companies. Microsoft, ExxonMobil (and its predecessor Standard Oil) and GE have dominated their markets and industries by focusing on their capacity to win every competition.

To find your moral attribute and get you on the way to finding your purpose, think about the following four sets of questions. Answer each, rate yourself according to the scale below, and total up each individual set of questions:

1 = no   2 = partially agree   3 = agree   4 = strongly agree   5 = boom, that's me

1. Could your purpose be driven by discovery?

1) Do you continually seek out the new, the innovative, and the meaningful, even in the face of adversity?

2) When you focus on something, do you pursue it relentlessly?

3) Would you say you remain steadfast in your convictions, and are willing to accept the consequences of your choices?

4) Do you look at each situation and opportunity with fresh eyes, and fearlessly invent your own response, without being burdened by the conventions of the past?

Write your total here:

2. Could your purpose be driven by excellence?

Would you say that ultimately you define and uphold your standards for your own reasons and they are not simply what is demanded by your customers?

Would you rather turn away customers than compromise the quality of your offering?

Would you say that you are creating a business more for your own fulfillment than anyone else's?

Is your commitment to reaching your ideal unwavering, despite setbacks or criticism?

Write your total here:

3. Could your purpose be driven by altruism?

Do you feel you exist primarily to serve your customers? ☐

Do you feel that your own happiness is measured by the happiness you bring to others? ☐

Is your focus on making people's lives, or the environment better? ☐

Does happiness take precedence over wealth in your eyes? ☐

Write your total here: ☐

4. Could your purpose be driven by heroism?

Do you have an obsession with winning? Do you feel driven to become the biggest and the best? ☐

Do you believe that "only some people are truly free so I will have to exercise my willpower and lead"? ☐

Does mediocrity frustrate you? ☐

Are you confident you have the necessary levels of courage, pride, and resilience to build a great brand? ☐

Write your total here: ☐

Which moral attribute did you score highest in? ☐

This is a good indication to where your purpose lies.

If you rated highest in No. 1, Discovery, this indicates your purpose has something to do with innovating within an industry. Discovery is rooted in the intuition that life is a kind of adventure. For example, at

Sony, the "joy of technological innovation" was explicitly stated by its founder as a reason for the company's existence.

Being a person who is on the search for the new your Purpose Statement could begin with:

- I want to the world to experience…

- I want to change…

- I want to create…

If you rated highest in No. 2, Excellence, this indicates your purpose might have something to do with providing the best possible product or service. Excellence built the Rolls Royce and some of today's most successful professional and creative businesses.

Brands that have a purpose based on excellence are Rolex, BMW, and Warren Buffett's firm Berkshire Hathaway. All have built their identity around the artistry of their endeavors. Businesses pursuing excellence would rather turn away customers than compromise their quality.

Creating the best is a priority for you so as a starting point, your Purpose Statement could begin with:

- I want to the world to experience the…

- I want to create the best…

- I want to see a world where…

- Everybody should…

If you rated highest in No. 3, Altruism, this indicates your purpose could have more to do with compassionate ambitions. Altruism is the driving force of any organization that exists primarily to help others, like many health organisations and charities.

Brands like Fedex, and even Target (Higher Quality, Lower Prices, Every Day), have established appeal around the idea that they are, first and foremost, making their customers happy. This takes the form of personal service beyond formal obligation, the provision of products at prices so low that they transform customers' lives, or the use of technology and ideas to improve human experience (like Hewlett-Packard and even Hallmark Cards).

As you are driven to make people happy, a starting point, your Purpose Statement could begin with:

- I want to create a world where…

- I want to help…

- I want to save…

If you rated highest in No. 4, Heroism, this indicates your purpose could be built around setting the standards and goals for everyone else to follow.

Travis Kalanick and his brand Uber fit into this camp perfectly. Described by those around him as a grinder, not a mogul, Kalanick's next-step plans are almost too huge to contemplate. Taking Uber into the world's biggest and toughest-to-crack markets of India and China; transforming Uber from "everyone's private driver" into a carpooling service; and then further reinventing itself—and how the world's cities operate—by introducing a fleet of autonomous vehicles.

Also think Microsoft's Bill Gates who has built machines that have changed the world and can claim that they had this purpose.

As you want to change industries and as you're driven to make the competition irrelevant your Purpose Statement could begin with:

- I want to change the way…

- I want to transform…

- I want to reinvent…

- I want to eradicate…

Tips for writing your purpose statement

When you're brainstorming and writing your purpose remember:

1. The statement should be personally fulfilling for you.

2. The statement should include how it will inspire your customers.

3. Finally, it should capture how your brand will have a positive impact on the world.

 For more help crafting your purpose download the 'Purpose" worksheets here: http://plan2brand. com/resources/worksheets/purpose

The key to a great purpose is to start with the greatest good. Don't tell your people and customers about what you want to see change in the business. State what you fundamentally believe must change in the world.

- Coke wants to see more happiness.

- Disney wants to see more magic.

- Virgin wants to see more rebellion.

- Google wants to see more things found.

- I want more small businesses to prosper.

What does your brand most want to see happen? What do you passionately want to see stop? Whatever you decide, that's the goal. And it should be one you are prepared to shout from the rooftops.

Remember – If your business needs general clarity or better traction for your marketing, if you want to feel stronger leading your team, try to find more clearly, and consistently articulate, your passions, desires and dreams. This belief in yourself will ignite the trust in people who see your passion and believe in your dreams.

Brand building example for 'Organic Fresh' – Purpose

Brand Foundations

Our Purpose
(the passion that gets us out of bed everyday!)

To help people stay healthy for longer by improving the quality of their food.

A word about research

If your product or service falls into the 'high consideration' class, that is, your prospects spend a decent amount of time researching and weighing up options prior to purchasing, then I recommend some form of research for the following two steps (Buyer Persona and Positioning). When deciding on your target consumer or business, or comparing yourself to the competition, it's not a great idea to make decisions based on your assumptions alone.

Whether it's original research, such as interviews, or desk research, such as government statistics, gathering and analysing information will give you insights many businesses fail to discover and leverage.

Gathering and analysing information will help you to:

- See trends and understand behaviors, motivations and factors that influence buyer decisions.

- Discover buyer insights that your competition doesn't know about.

- Create a Buyer Persona that becomes the focus of your marketing, where your content becomes the crossroads between what they want to hear and what you want to say.

- Brief marketers, creative designers, copywriters and your sales people so they deliver messages that are relevant to your prospects.

When it comes to gathering information, you have two basic options:

Existing research - easy to access from existing data.

Original research - can be harder to access; takes time and effort.

Let's look at a summary of both options and a few resources you can use.

Existing Research

1) Internal Data

This is where you look at your sales figures, profit and loss statements, customer profiles, notes on conversations with customers or prospects, returns, previous marketing campaigns for insights.

2) Your Website Analytics

Analytic software can offer you a great deal of information about who accesses your site. Once you have installed a tracking code, you can look at metrics such as page traffic, referring sites, conversion rates, search engine traffic, social media leads, sales revenue, bounce rates, mobile traffic and conversion rates.

3) Social Media

There is a wealth of information you can access through forums, analytics, keyword research and by following activity in your sphere to observe what people are saying.

There are also a number of social media monitoring tools you can use such as:

Sysomos (https://sysomos.com/)

Klear (http://klear.com/)

Followerwonk (https://moz.com/followerwonk/) – Twitter only

Sum All (https://sumall.com/)

Simply Measured (http://bit.ly/1RVFXKz)

For specific analytics look at your Twitter and Facebook.

4) Public Statistical Sources

A great deal of information, particularly demographic information, can be found through public resources such as industry bodies, government agencies, libraries and local councils. Here are some examples for Australia. For other countries you will need to do a Google Search.

Australian Bureau of Statistics (http://www.abs.gov.au/)

IBIS World (http://www.ibisworld.com.au/) – access to data from over 700 industries in Australia

Sensis business report (http://bit.ly/1orwBif) – insight on the Australian business landscape

Australian Small Business (http://bit.ly/1SK01CY) – Key statistics and analysis

Statistics Australia http://bit.ly/1Y7rNdV) – key national indicators, census data for Australia

5) Google

You may find out some interesting information just by doing a general Google search. For example, a quick search can reveal which is the 'most popular mobile app with millennials', or 'how much Australians spend on food each year'. Whatever information you feel could help add detail to your Buyer Persona, it's always a good idea to try and find out if it already exists somewhere out there.

Original Research

By far the most time consuming way to go but conducting your own interviews can be the best way to gain insights that statistics just don't deliver. Think about the following options:

1) Build a picture from your own experience

Get together anyone who is customer facing and compile your assumptions about the problems people are trying to solve, and what their motivations are, in terms of the functional or emotional benefits they seek.

2) Focus groups

Typically a group of 8-12 people who are brought together to have an in-depth discussion about an offering so that insights can be gained that would otherwise not be known. A moderator facilitates and asks questions to guide the discussion. A downside of this process is that, in a group format, some people will give answers that they think you want to hear rather than their actual opinion, or they will simply go along with the group. It can also be cost prohibitive for some businesses, but this should be weighed against the valuable insights you might gain that could give you a competitive advantage.

3) Customer and non-customer surveys

These can be done in several ways; by emailing an interactive PDF, by phone, a plug-in via your website, or on old fashioned paper! Good surveys have a combination of short, multiple choice questions, alongside more leading, open-ended questions. The aim is to get general data such as age, gender etc. alongside insightful information on motivations and behaviors.

It can be difficult to get people to fill them in, so there are techniques you can use such as giveaways, discounts or competitions.

Online surveys can be useful for getting a snapshot of information that can be gathered in a cost effective way. There are a few survey software options (see 2016 Best Survey Software reviews) that you can incorporate onto your website.

4) Interviews

Done well, this is the best way to get the most credible insights from customers and prospects. Interviews are not sales calls, but are a fact-finding mission. It's a real conversation where you listen to what prompted them to make their decisions. The downside to this method is time consuming and you need to be confident in conversing and listening intently at the same time – an art in itself.

Step 2

Identify your ideal customer

"We used to put the brand in the middle. Now the consumer is smack-dab in the middle of everything we do. And that means we need to understand who our customer is."
– Joaquin Hidalgo, brand CMO, Nike

Step 2: Identify your ideal customer

One fundamental problem most businesses have when formulating a brand strategy is the inability to really look at what they are doing from an outside perspective. That is the perspective of the consumer. To get noticed today you need to understand your audience's top concerns so you can address their problems and base your marketing messages around solving their wants and needs.

Have you ever looked at an ad and said, "I don't get it, why would I want that?" Or conversely, seen one that felt like it was made just for you? In the first case, either you weren't part of that product's target market, or worse, they didn't understand how to market to you. In the second case, they 'got' you and had developed their message to speak directly to you and others like you.

There's no doubt that success today is dictated by having your message seen by your target customer, but the more it pulls on their heartstrings by speaking to them emotionally, the better your chance of gaining their attention.

The problem for all of us is that getting noticed is getting harder every day. It's estimated that we've gone from seeing 500 marketing messages a day in the 1980's to now being bombarded by over 5000+ a day. So to reach your potential customers and get them to devote what little attention they can (see highlight Gaining your prospects attention has never been harder) to considering your product or service, your marketing message needs to be targeted, precise and relevant. Oh, and very succinct.

Gaining your prospect's attention has never been harder

In the digital age, where the news is shared in 140 characters and conversations take place in the form of emojis, our prospect's attention span has shortened significantly.

In a recent 54-page study, Microsoft sought to understand what impact technology and today's digital lives were having on attention spans. The researchers collected data from surveys of more than 2,000 people to determine the impact of pocket-sized devices and the increased availability of digital media and information were having on everyday life.

The findings revealed our attention span has fallen from an average of 12 seconds in the year 2000 to just 8 seconds today. That's shorter than a goldfish (9 seconds average).

Buyer Persona

To discover the messages that make your prospects think 'hey, they get me,' you should be creating a *Buyer Persona*. A Buyer Persona is a fictional character that represents your ideal prospect. It's an in-depth composite of the characteristics, behaviors, and motivations of your ideal customer. When complete, it will help you understand the motivating beliefs, fears and secret desires that influence your customers as they work through the process of considering, and then purchasing a product or service like yours.

Now you might say, "But do I really need to spend a lot of time creating a Buyer Persona?" If that's the case, think about the alternatives, what are you going to do? Start advertising anywhere and everywhere, throwing money around and hoping something will stick? And what exactly are you going to say? What's going to cut through? What can you highlight that demonstrates the difference between you and your competitors? Yes, you can guess at it but to get it right takes time. And that's what this second step in the process is about, understanding what the customer wants, and not simply selling or marketing what your service or product does.

What's in it for me?

A prospective buyer is always thinking about "What's in it for me?" We've moved on from the time when marketing was all about the product. It was simpler pre-internet days. Marketing could just talk about what features a product or service had. Today it's all about the customer and customization, which means you should thinking about 'making what the customer wants, not making customers want what you make'. And you can only do that if you have an intimate understanding of your buyer.

> "Today you should be thinking more about making what the customer wants, not making customers want what you make."

The fact is, your business starts when you have a customer, not a product, and to be successful today you should be able to answer:

- What problem does my customer need solved?

- What benefit do I deliver to them by solving it?

- How will I solve it better than others?

- Why should they trust me?

"Get closer than ever to your customer. So close that you tell them what they need well before they realize it themselves."
– Steve Jobs

The insights a well-researched *Buyer Persona* give you will not only help improve your marketing messages, it also gets you thinking about what you could potentially fine tune or change within your business, so you're putting distance between you and your competitors. Remember, all of these exercises are about finding and describing a point of difference.

How understanding your target market makes a difference

In America, Chipotle Mexican Grill is certainly the most innovative fast food company today, and since its launch 23 years ago, has held firm to its bold brand promise: Food with Integrity.

Their growth and profits have been described as 'phenomenal' and consistently among the highest in the fast-food industry, despite the high cost of the raw ingredients and labor required to maintain their promise of integrity.

How is that possible?

It comes down to a simple brand strategy that drives nearly every business decision they make. Chipotle understands their target market intimately.

Chipotle targets millennials exclusively. To connect emotionally with them, they offer the healthiest and freshest fast food available. They understand millennials don't trust traditional advertising, so they avoid mass media and pushy sales tactics.

To promote the brand, they work at a more grassroots level through initiatives like their Cultivate Food Music Festival and their Farm Team Loyalty Program — both focused on humane food sourcing and organic farming.

In a nutshell, Chipotle's brand strategy was to get inside their target customer's heads by studying their likes and dislikes, and building a strategy that appealed to them.

The reality is, while this strategy is different than that of their larger competitors, it's not so unconventional or unique. Yet it's created a company with a projected revenue of more than $4.5 billion for 2016.

If you don't have a clear picture of your target market, you may find that you differentiate your brand the wrong way. You need to make sure your differences are attracting your ideal customers.

Chipotle's decision to laser target a market with distinct needs and wants isn't so revolutionary. The real magic happens for any brand when their target market feels like **'they get me.'**

Smaller businesses, start-ups and new ideas often fail, not because the idea or the business is wrong, but because gaining a critical understanding of the real target market through a Buyer Persona is given a low priority.

To connect at a more human level, businesses need to use marketing messages that engage with their customers at a more emotional level.

An example of emotional connection

Many people are unaware that in 1999, well before the release of the iPod, RCA developed a very sophisticated MP3 player they named Lyra. RCA's advertising focused on features and performance, and sales were dismal. One of their core marketing messages was '1 GB of storage'.

On October 23, 2001, Apple lifted the curtain on their version of the MP3, the iPod.

Notably, Apple's marketing didn't focus on features. The visually memorable 'dancing silhouettes' and the simple promotional line, **'1000 songs in your pocket',** was the strategy that changed the music industry. Apple's research told them that their target market wasn't turned on by the fact that a music device had 1 GB of storage, they wanted to carry their music with them!

Advertising that makes a customer feel like 'they get me' is hands down more persuasive and one of the most important keys to a brand's success.

Your Buyer Persona

To develop the marketing messages that make your prospects feel like 'they get me' you must create an insightful Buyer Persona.

While challenging, this is the most important foundation of your brand foundations. As a small business, you can't be all things to all people. With limited resources, it makes sense to service a smaller, specific group of consumers or, in the case of B2Bs, certain types of businesses, exceptionally well.

To connect emotionally with your prospects you must understand the challenges, wants and the desires that affect their buying choice. This is especially important for purchases of medium to high consideration products/services, where the dynamics behind the selection and buying decision can be more complex, as opposed to a low consideration offering, such as a magazine or chocolate bar.

This is where you want to be able to put yourself in your prospects shoes. You should be trying to identify the things your potential buyers say to themselves when they are evaluating an offering like yours. I don't mean an academic understanding. I mean, learning exactly what they say to themselves as the move through the buying process. This is where powerful marketing messages begin to emerge and it's not something you can guess at.

To do this we've developed a process where you conduct a small series of interviews to help unearth insights into five key areas.

This process of creating an insightful buyer persona is more successful when you conduct some real buyer interviews yourself.

 If you have what is considered a high consideration product or service, and you want to follow our interview steps to truly get into your buyers head, you can download our eBook that guides you through the process here: **http://plan2brand.com/resources/worksheets/buyerpersona**

It explains how you can develop a more valuable and insightful Buyer Persona, by building it around the story behind buyers actual considerations, deliberations, expectations and concerns.

The process we have created was inspired by the methodology developed by 25 year marketing veteran Adele Revella (https://www.amazon.com/Adele-Revella/e/B00R05WN58).

How to create awesome Buyer Insights without interviewing

The second best option for 'getting inside' their heads is to rely on your own knowledge, insights or assumptions, and do your best answering the following questions.

To do this you need to step outside your business, and put yourself into your buyers shoes, and think about what issues occupy their mind as they search for a solution, to a burning problem or top priority, as it relates to the purchase of your product or service. This is how it works.

Brainstorming and creating Buying Insights for your Buyer Persona:

Using these steps you're aiming to form a clear picture of the evaluation process your prospects go through as they search for a solution. Your prospects evaluation process has five stages that you need to gain a better understanding of.

The five Drivers for Buying Insights are:

1) Their Solution Triggers: Here you are trying to identify what business conditions or personal circumstances trigger your prospects to spend time and energy looking for a new solution?

2) Their Critical Must Haves: The must haves are the most critical features your prospects need, so they feel confident your offering will work for their circumstances?

3) Their Desired Outcomes: The results or outcomes you are looking for, whether tangible (rational benefits) or intangible (emotional benefits) are the things your prospects expect from a solution like yours?

4) Their Likely Roadblocks: The roadblocks are the likely attitudes, perceptions or concerns they may have that could stop them buying? and;

5) Their Buyer Journey: This is all about the process they follow and what resources they look for to explore and select a solution?

As you work through this process the key is to write in buyer's language. Think about what language or phrases they would 'actually' use in a conversation with a friend, not a sales person? Try to avoid industry jargon (unless they would use it), superlatives or formal tone.

The steps go as follows:

Write some Buyer Knowledge Quotes (BKQ's) as short statements of what buyers might say for all five of the Drivers for Buying Insights

Your BKQ's should sound natural. After you've created between 5-10, group similar BKQ's, look at your brainstormed 'quotes' and see if you can group up to three with similar 'insight' or 'sentiment' into a set.

Now look at the sets of BKQ's to see if you can identify the main need/idea in each set as a singular short statement or Key Insight Headline. These statements are important as they can be used in the development of marketing messages or activities.

Reverse brainstorm. If it's easier, reverse your brainstorm by thinking of a word or phrase that could be part of a KIH, for example 'ease of use'. Think about where buyers want 'ease of use' to create more specific BKQ's combined with a compelling KIH.

As you move through the five Drivers for Buying Insights below there are examples to demonstrate what you are trying to achieve. Good luck.

1)   **Their Solution Triggers**

Brainstorm what business conditions or personal circumstances trigger your buyers to look for a new solution? Identify the 3-5 objectives or problems they are dedicating time to.

Try thinking about what's really on your buyer's radar? You don't want to arrogantly presume, just because your solution fixes something, that your buyer will also be obsessed with this. They may have other priorities that are keeping them awake at night, so think about what those might be.

For instance, if you were a bicycle retailer, you want to identify what triggered a prospect to walk into your store? Would your Buyer Insights look something like this:

Most of my friends ride and they all rave about how fit they feel and how the team elements helps inspire them so much.

I started riding with a group and it amazed me how often they all catch up after riding and how close they all are.

My girlfriend thinks it's great that I have such a close group of friends that I see 3 times a week.

If these insights were true, when you group them together, a potential Key Insight Headline could be:

The social aspect of bike riding really appeals to me.

Now if you step back, could that knowledge help you in your marketing or social media? What would an insight like that mean to your strategy?

When you begin to understand these triggers you can define, defend and execute strategies that resonate with buyers at the earliest stages in their decision. Your content can tell them "You may not have experienced this yet, but it's coming soon. Here's how to avoid it"

Prompter questions to help you with brainstorming your Solution Trigger buying insights:

What was the trigger (objective or pain) that prompted buyers to look for a solution?

What circumstances changed to make it a priority to start looking?

What would buyers do first to evaluate options, e.g. internet search, talk to peers?

2) Their Critical Must Haves (what, how)

Brainstorm what top 3-5 benchmarks do buyers use to evaluate/compare alternative approaches to a problem? What features are critical to achieve their 'Desired Outcomes'?

All buyers have a specific set of requirements, but as they go through the evaluation process and become more educated, they begin to refine or alter their decision criteria.

When you think about your type of solution, what attributes do you think they would compare to others? Which ones do they care about the most and why? If we go back to the bicycle retailer example, a common insight could be:

I'm a bit concerned about how much money I'll have to spend on maintaining the bike.

It's a pretty expensive sport and I really need to get to grips with doing the little repairs and maintenance myself.

I've heard it's really important to keep an elite bike in tip top condition and I'm not sure how I'll do that yet.

If these insights were true, when you group them together, a potential Key Insight Headline could be:

I want to know how to look after the bike equipment myself.

Headline quotes like the one above can be invaluable when it comes to thinking about your services, marketing messages and content. And they are critical for sales enablement, as they identify which features you think buyers really care about and why.

Prompter questions to help you brainstorm your Critical Must Have Buying Insights:

What do you think buyers perceive to be the most critical capabilities of your type of solution, service or product (e.g. specific features, implementation issues, price v value calculations)?

What aspects of your type of solution do buyers think as relevant and irrelevant?

What do buyers not compromise on or trade off?

What facts (not benefits) would buyers like to know about your type of solution so they are more likely to trust you/ buy from you?

3) Their Desired Outcomes (why)

Brainstorm what results or outcomes, whether tangible (rational benefits) or intangible (emotional benefits), you think your buyers expect from a solution like yours?

Desired Outcomes resemble benefits, but not like the ones that can be reverse engineered from the capabilities your solution delivers.

A tangible outcome might be a metric for growth, or cost savings, or an intangible outcome might be a social gain, or positive emotions like feeling healthier. Whatever it is, there will be something at stake – a wrong decision could result in a job loss, your prospects may want to widen their sphere of influence, or control something in their environment. What outcome is of most value to them and why?

Let's look at the bicycle retailer again. An emotional benefit could come from these three buyer insights.

Each time I get on my bike it's a new experience each time.

I love getting up at the crack of dawn when no one else is around and on my bike with my thoughts. It's my own form of meditation.

I never know what I'm going to see on my bike, it's always different and things that I wouldn't normally take notice of if I was in my car.

If these insights were true, when you group them together, a potential Key Insight Headline could be:

A bike gives me freedom to explore and have new experiences.

Desired Outcomes and Critical Must Haves can be confused. Desired Outcomes are scenarios that the buyer believes will change after they have purchased. By contrast, Critical Must Haves are about the solutions capabilities. These are the 'what' and 'how' factors, where as Desired Outcomes answers 'why' an aspect of a solution is important. In this case, the emotional feeling of freedom and exploring is an intangible outcome that could be more important than price!

Prompter questions to help you brainstorm your buying insights:

What do buyers expect to change if they bought a solution, product or service like yours?

What are the positive social consequences they desire (e.g. status, look good, feel empowered, in control)?

What would go beyond a buyer's expectations (e.g. high service level, quality, payment plan)?

What savings are buyers looking for (e.g. money, time, effort)?

What would make a buyer's 'job' easier (e.g. flatter learning curve, low running cost, ease of use, simple design)?

What emotional benefits come from an aspect of the solution, product or service? (e.g. get lots of support – feel empowered)

4)   Their Likely Roadblocks

Brainstorm what attitudes or concerns prevent buyers from investing in a solution like yours? Or, why would they buy from a competitor instead of from you?

This can be overlooked because it's the 'bad news' – the things you don't talk about, or consider.

Where are the barriers or negative impressions of your business/ type of solution coming from? Buyer's perceptions may come from a peer, an expert, or a prior experience. Sometimes these things are not factually correct but can prevent them from buying.

Using a bicycle retailer example again, some buyer Insights could be:

> *A lot of the bike shops here have the same common brands and I expected more choice, especially the latest European and American ones.*
>
> *I see some amazing bikes online, but you just don't seem to be able to get them here, let alone test ride them.*
>
> *Every shop seems to carry the same brands in Australia. They are fine but I've seen some really cool bikes online.*

If these insights were true, when you group them together, a potential Key Insight Headline could be:

> *I want a lot more choice when buying a new bicycle.*

As a result of knowing these barriers, your content would focus on 'overcoming and addressing this objections' (ones that your competition didn't even know about) and possibly changing something within your business that addresses the problem. Interviewing would give you the best insights here, but give it a go!

Prompter questions to help you brainstorm your buying insights:

> *What concerns do they have that would prevent you from investing in your offering (e.g. biases, attitudes, perceptions about your business – whether accurate or not)?*
>
> *What are the major factors that prevent buyers from changing/adopting a new solution (e.g. contract lock-in, Government regulations, existing good customer service, great value, lack of funds)?*

What are common objections from other decision makers that may influence buyers?

5) Their Buyer Journey

Brainstorm what process buyers follow and what resources do they explore in their search for a solution? What is the buyer's role and impact of others in the purchase decision?

This stage is about the behind-the-scenes story of what buyers do to evaluate and eliminate options and settle on their final choice. What resources do buyers trust to answer their questions?

Who is involved and what role do they play in the decision? There could be a complex ecosystem of characters and it's not always the 'lead' decision maker who has the most clout.

Continuing our bicycle retailer scenario one part of a buyer's journey could be reflected in these insights.

I won't trust a Facebook ad or some website. I got a few recommendations from friends and then went into the stores to suss them out and see if they really knew their stuff.

My wife said I should buy it online, it would be cheaper. I thought about that but it was really hard to compare all of the features and there really is a lot involved in choosing a bike today.

If these insights were true, when you group them together, a potential Key Insight Headline could be:

I'm looking for an expert who can help me compare equipment.

These Buyer Journey findings can help you audit your current content's usefulness and identify gaps. You need your marketing and sales resources readily available to answer buyer's specific questions, when and where they are needed.

Prompter questions to help you brainstorm your buying insights:

What primary sources of information do buyers trust (e.g. work colleagues, friends, family, peers)?

What secondary sources of information would buyers use (e.g. Facebook, blogs, forums, websites, industry sites)?

Who impacts the decision and in what way (e.g. user, influencer, purse strings, agitator)?

What stages are there to the evaluation/elimination process (wide search, narrow to a few options, demo, group discussions)?

What would help buyers make their decision to keep or eliminate you from their list of potentials?

What do buyers envisage as being a successful sale and post-sales experience?

Case Study

I had a participant in one of my workshops who was building a brand that sold women's yoga clothes online. Naturally she was experiencing trouble getting traction and growing with competitors like Nike and Lululemon.

Her product was already different from the competition, but she was not clear on the pain she was alleviating for her target market. The clothing range had extra items not normally available in typical yoga stores, such as tops and throw-overs that matched the yoga clothing. As she thought through the Buyer Persona exercises above it became clear that her target market's desired outcomes was saving time. This helped her to define her target market as 'forty-plus women who value their time'.

This revelation changed everything for her. Suddenly she was able to think more clearly about why she was producing the range she had been designing instinctively, almost by default. She was actually designing clothes for women like herself who were time-poor but wanted to fit a lot of important things into their day. The matching range of light coats and throws allowed women to get to yoga, then catch up with friends for a quick coffee, go to work and meet a prospective customer for lunch, all without a change of clothes.

Step 3

Position yourself for success

"If you don't have a point of difference, you'd better have a low price." – Jack Trout

Step 3: Position yourself for success

Growing a brand is all about perceptions, so in order to gain a positive reputation and be perceived well by consumers, your brand needs to be well positioned in the mind of your customer.

By following this seven step process, your purpose will be starting to take shape, and you're clearer on your prospect's needs and wants. The next step is to focus on 'finding a differentiated position for your product or service' so you stand apart from your competition in a meaningful way.

Positioning is the place in the consumer's mind that you want your brand to own. It is the benefit that you want your consumer to perceive when they think of your brand.

For instance, I think you would agree Mercedes owns the 'luxury' position within the car market, and BMW owns the 'performance' position.

It important to note that it isn't enough merely to be different from the competition. It's important to be different from the competition in ways that matter to your market. If your target market (think Buyer Persona) is concerned about the environment, informing them of your ecologically friendly manufacturing processes is obviously going to be great idea if your competition doesn't have the same process.

To thrive and grow in today's competitive landscape you need to find spaces in your market for which there are fewer or no direct competitors. It is a different approach from the traditional attempts of beating the competition with price and quality improvement wars. And because our brains love to find things that are new, unusual or unexpected – a brand that is unique will grab attention and have an advantage over its competition.

When your brand position fulfills the following three key criteria, you will achieve the elevator effect we are all chasing.

Different

People nowadays are constantly faced with a barrage of choices. As Marty Neumeier, the author of '*The Brand Gap*' and '*Zag*' states: "The overabundance of similar products and services is forcing people to look for something that is different and will separate winners from all this clutter." Critical to creating a successful business today is using strategy and innovation to stand apart from your competitors.

Focused

If businesses just expand their product and service range to try to attract more customers, everyone ends up offering the same as each other, resulting in commoditisation. Once your products and services are considered to be a commodity, the only way to compete will be on price and your margins are going to suffer.

However, focus on the right niche, or better yet create a new niche where you are regarded as being the leading expert, and you'll attract customers who are willing to pay a premium for your specialist services and products.

Relevant

If you're not relevant, then you aren't really in business. Even if your company is differentiated and specialised, if nobody needs or is willing to buy your product, you won't last. This is why you need to carry out research to figure out if people are interested in your proposed or existing business and specialty. Success comes when you discover what your customers' pains and needs are and you can offer a solution to them.

"Positioning is not what you do to the product; it's what you do to the mind of the prospect. It compensates for our over-communicated society by using an oversimplified message to cut through the clutter and get into the mind. Positioning focuses on the perceptions of the prospect, not on the reality of the brand." - Al Ries, marketing expert and co-author of 'Positioning: The Battle For Your Mind'

Let's begin

Following are two fundamental ways you can unearth your 'point of difference.'

Note: in my workshops and consulting we often go much deeper using tools and processes that don't translate well into the written word.

When we look at differentiating a business from its competitors, we are looking at either one of two possible scenarios:

1) The company exists and may have strengths and differentiators - we just have to find and articulate them.

2) The company is new and planning to create a product or service that is differentiated or it's an existing brand that wants to completely reposition itself.

If you're in the first camp read on. If you're in the second camp jump to page 108 and complete Exercise 2.

Exercise 1

There are two parts to this exercise:

1) Compare yourself against your competition to look for opportunities for your differentiation.

2) Look for your company's existing point of difference or competitive advantage to identify points of difference.

Step 1

The aim of this first exercise is to look at your existing strengths and identify the points of difference that set you apart from your competitors. You should consider doing some research for this exercise.

Note: for a detailed list of 22 ways to differentiate jump to page 171.

I encourage my clients to identify at least three competitors and then choose the most appropriate comparison criteria for your situation (see a suggested list below). Then it's a case of comparing yourself to your competitors and rating yourself against your competition (1 being low or poor, and 5 being very good).

BUSINESS RELATED CRITERIA		BRAND RELATED CRITERIA
• Product/service quality • Product/service uniqueness • Product/service features • Product/service effectiveness • Customer service • Price • Innovation	• Market share • Distribution channels/power • Brand awareness/ name recognition • Reputation • Corporate citizenship • Financial strength • Sales ability • Environmental responsibility	• Overall presentation (brand) • Overall presentation (www) • Immediate messaging impressions • Taglines/slogans - (clear, to the point?) • Quality of images/ graphics • Positioning/clear point of difference? • 'Cool' factor

Below, Table 3.1 shows you an example of a competition comparison chart.

Criteria	You	Comp. 1	Comp. 2	Comp. 3
Price	2	4	3	3
Customer service	4	2	2	2
Distribution channels/power	3	3	3	5
Innovation	5	3	2	2
Guarantee	5	0	0	0
Product/service uniqueness	4	4	3	3
Product/service effectiveness	5	3	3	2
Product/service quality	4	3	2	4

Table 3.1

By completing an exercise similar to the one shown in Table 3.1 you can see straight away where you score better than average or worse than average. You might see some categories where everybody gets a low score. What opportunities are there if that is the case? Is there potential to improve your performance and create a differentiation in some area? Would it be worth doing?

Step 2

The next step is to look for your company's existing point of difference or competitive advantage *from your customer's point of view.*

To do this, complete the following three steps below and refer to table 3.2 to see how to do this exercise.

Step 1 – For each of the strengths you identified in *Step 1*, rate how important that feature is to the client in column A.

Step 2 – Next, rate each strength based on your ability to beat the competition.

Step 3 – Add column A and B to get your total rating.

List your strengths, the things you are most competent at and the features or resource your product or service provides	A Value to client (1-10)	B Versus comp. (1-10)	Total Score A+B
Money back guarantee	7	1	8
Superior track record - 20+ years successfully trading	6	5	11
Unique patent/process that delivers above the industry standard	6	4	10
Free support and training for one year	8	8	16
The largest range in the industry	7	6	13
Specialist knowledge that the competitors can't currently match	6	5	11

Table 3.2

This exercise will help you to compare your strongest brand assets against your competitors, score them and look for the one or two strengths that score the highest and stand out. These are your points of difference!

You should look at these differentiators critically. Can you enhance them in some way? How can you highlight them? Where would be the best place to mention them on your website, in a conversation, in a sales letter?

Remember that any claim you make you must be able to substantiate either by specific details or evidence. Where possible verify the facts or write 'proof points' for each differentiator or claim. You can't claim that you have the best quality control if you can't provide your ISO9001-2000 certificate or similar support for your claim.

The reality is that establishing and maintaining any sort of differentiation or competitive advantage is an ongoing challenge. What differentiates you today can be copied tomorrow. Your product or service offering, through to your messaging and marketing campaigns, will all be affected by changing economic conditions and the evolving market place. You will need to keep refining, updating, and renewing your position in the market regularly.

Above all, differentiation can and must be created, or you will be forever seen as a commodity and forced to compete on price.

Exercise 2

If you're in the exciting position of creating a new product or service, or you're looking to make a major change or shift to your existing brand, the following exercise is more appropriate.

Terrain mapping

To ensure the success of any brand transformation or creation, you need to find the right position for your brand, and the best tool for this is often referred to as 'terrain mapping' or 'competitive landscaping.' This kind of exercise is commonly used to brainstorm competitive positioning, and by judiciously creating a range of terrain maps, it can help you to find a completely new position in your market place.

Pretty much the Holy Grail for any business today!

A terrain map exercise consists of an x and y axis (horizontal and vertical). The principal is to measure yourself, using the axis, against your competitors according to features and benefits that matter to your prospects. The aim is to find a place within your market where there is little to no competition.

To give you an idea of how this exercise works below is an example from Apple.

Image 3.3 is from a terrain map that I imagined would have helped Apple justify the development of the iPad. When mapping Apple products and the competition along two axis that represented Price (high versus low) and Technology (Enthusiasts versus Pragmatists), one clear market gap appears.

Enthusiasts are those who need a powerful device to not only consume, but also create content, such as designers, video editors, professional gamers, musicians, and so forth. Pragmatists are those who just consume the available content and are not interested in actively creating it.

High Performance Laptops and Desktops (developed for design, video processing and high-memory applications) fit into the top left quadrant and appeal to the technology enthusiasts. Smartphones sit in the middle on the technology scale – along with medium-price and medium-high performance notebooks designed for activities such as word and spreadsheet processing. Individual entertainment devices – such as e-readers and portable video games and DVD players – suit the pragmatist but generally only perform one function.

Through a process like this Apple would have seen a gap in the market, a need for a product smaller than a laptop, larger than an iPhone, and suitable for the pragmatists. This is known in the marketing industry as 'uncontested space.'

As Apple undoubtedly did, you will need to try several different axis options, using a mix relevant to your customers, before you discover one that sparks real insight.

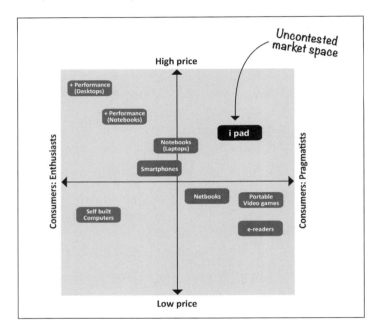

Image 3.3

Creating your terrain map

Begin your terrain map by drawing an x and y axis (one travelling east-west, and the other travelling north-south), and an A3 piece of paper. Now follow these steps:

1. Identify all of your direct and indirect competitors.

2. Using a horizontal and vertical axis, plot a number of explicit and implicit axes of differentiation, qualitative or quantitative.

3. Place each of your competitors on your chart in the space that best describes their market position.

4. Identify the areas where most competitors are focused.

5. Look for 'empty spaces' where a combination of features fills an unmet need.

6. Identify which consumer segments could be interested in your new found (often counter-intuitive) combination of features.

7. Determine if the market segment is financially viable.

8. Ask yourself if your business has the capability to adapt and offer such a product and at what cost.

9. Establish viability by pricing your new niche, addressing distribution/delivery issues and developing an advertising strategy which aims to deliver the product profitably.

10. Consider patents as you find ways to establish your new market quickly and defend the niche against 'invaders.'

You can draw up your own axes or download the instruction sheet here.

 Unlock your terrain map exercise here: http:// plan2brand.com/resources/worksheets/ terrainmap

As you work through the exercise, remember:

1. The axis must relate to things that are important to the customer, not you. Identify the function that most customers of your segment find important.

2. Don't just look at direct competitors. Look for companies who are capable of addressing the same customer needs you do. If you sell floorboards, look at tiling shops and think of *all* the needs your prospects hope to address with your product.

3. The key to finding uncontested territory with one of these maps is deciding which values to assign to your x – y axis. The obvious axis are physical attributes like price or availability, but make sure you explore things like emotional benefits. If your product is food, consider things like 'physical fulfillment' versus 'emotional wellbeing.' By defaulting to very standard categories such as price/quality (high-price and low-price versus high-quality and low-quality), you won't find any breakthroughs of value.

A positioning checklist

A new differentiated position is most powerful when it represents a single idea. If you can tick off the following, you will have found the right positioning:

* You're unique in your marketplace – true differentiation.

* You're the best in your niche.

* You stir up the competition.

* You're clear on your target market.

- You're consistent but always evolving.

- You provoke, make a noise, and you get noticed.

Terrain mapping for generic businesses

Fully repositioning your business is a huge challenge. When it comes to generic or vanilla businesses, such as accountants, chiropractors, hairdressers, and so on, terrain mapping may not give you the 'eureka' moment demonstrated by the iPad example. However, going through the exercise can highlight to you just how similar your business is to your competition and demonstrating the importance of thinking about your differentiation.

If you have a generic business, begin your terrain mapping exercise by simply writing down **what you are, or can be, best at.** From there it becomes a case of accentuating that aspect of your business.

For instance, you might be a florist with a secret passion for native flora. You could find out how many florists sell only native flowers, investigate the financial implications, and do some research into the potential size of the market. It makes sense to niche in a market that you love.

A narrow niche is great when it comes to getting found through online search. By having a business that can be found using what the industry calls a 'long-tail keyword' (in the case of the florist the long-tail keyword would be 'native-flower florist') there is less competition and these kinds of keywords are cheaper to purchase if you're using adwords to find customers.

The Blue Ocean Strategy

The ultimate in differentiating your business (think of it as terrain mapping on steroids) is an extreme concept called the 'Blue Ocean Strategy'. Renee Mauborgne and W. Chan Kim, who published their groundbreaking book, 'Blue Ocean Strategy', in 2005, pioneered this concept. In it they argue that you can reach new customers and make your competition completely irrelevant by following their methodology of *creating* uncontested markets. It's a great read for any business.

In their book they theorise that there are two types of business oceans in this world. The first is the red business ocean, which is full of rivals and extremely competitive. It's common for businesses to find themselves in this space, which has been made bloody by too many combative rivalries and a level of competition that requires cutthroat tactics to keep your head above water. The pressure to compete on price is inevitable and surviving in this space, let alone growing, is very difficult.

The blue ocean, however, is the opposite of the red ocean. It is a place that represents uncontested new market spaces where the lack of competition almost guarantees growth. A blue ocean strategy works because it creates demand instead of fighting for space.

Most businesses just assume there will be competition, that it's the nature of business today, right? Not necessarily. It's possible to *create* a blue ocean.

Two ways to create blue oceans

There are two ways to create a blue ocean business. One is to build a completely new industry or segment – think eBay and the online auction industry.

The second and more common way, which can be utilised by existing companies, is to create a blue ocean by working from within a red ocean to alter its boundaries. This is what Cirque du Soleil did by breaking through the boundary traditionally separating circus and theatre. It hit the Ringling Bros and Barnum & Bailey square in the jaw at a time when the traditional circus business was in long-term decline.

Founded in 1984 by a group of talented street performers, Cirque's first tagline was 'We reinvent the circus.' Their unique offering pulled in an entirely new audience. By broadening their appeal to adults, they created a differentiated proposition, making the competition irrelevant. The lucrative corporate market who traditionally frequented the ballet, theatre or the opera became their audience.

Cirque achieved global success in a very short time by not challenging conventional logic. Instead of offering a better solution by creating a circus experience with more fun and action, they completely reinvented the offering by adding the intellectual sophistication and artistic values of theatre.

Where to once you've found a better place to position your brand?

When you have found a way to position your brand and stand apart in your market, you need to share it with your team so they can tell your customers about it! And the best tool to do that is referred to as your **Positioning Statement**. A Positioning Statement is a statement developed for your staff and stakeholders that outlines the unique benefits that your company promises to deliver to its customers every time they interact with your brand. Your Positioning Statement summarises your core selling idea. It is an internal statement intended to create focus, priority, and clarity about the company's goals, unique value propositions and culture now that you're unique to the competition.

A Positioning Statement serves as the foundation on which you can build all of your messaging and leads you to your business promise.

As a differentiator, a Positioning Statement is a must, but few businesses have one. Businesses are often either unaware of the concept or fail to invest time and energy to develop one because they can be hard to quantify, measure and guarantee.

The addition of an engaging Positioning Statement will help your business to:

- Clearly determine your strategic goals.

- Develop a results-driven plan to achieve your goals.

- Build a fully aligned and coordinated brand that knows exactly how to meet unmet, or under-met needs in the market.

- Set the foundations and benchmarks for a differentiated product and/or service offering.

- Accelerate market success.

Developing your Positioning Statement

To begin developing your Positioning Statement you can follow the formula commonly used by many popular brands. It's based on answering the following four deceptively simple questions:

- Who is your target market?

- What is the frame of reference?

- What is your point of differentiation?

- How can you justify your claim?

To see a Positioning Statement in action, below is one from Federal Express and one from Amazon. You can see how both brand's promises have been formulated by answering the four questions in the formula.

Amazon

Amazon.com strives to be Earth's most customer-centric company where people can find and discover virtually anything they want to buy online. By giving customers more of what they want - low prices, vast selection, and convenience - Amazon.com continues to grow and evolve as a world-class e-commerce platform.

Breaking this down into the four elements of a brand promise/positioning statement, you see:

Target market = People who want to buy online
Frame of reference = E-commerce platform
Differentiation = Most customer-centric company
Justification = Low prices, vast selection, convenience

> ### Federal Express
>
> To deadline-oriented business people, Federal Express is the overnight package delivery service that is the most reliable because of its sophisticated package tracking system.
>
> Breaking this down into the four elements of a brand promise/positioning statement, you see:
>
> **Target market =** Deadline-oriented business people
> **Frame of reference =** Overnight package delivery service
> **Differentiation** = The most reliable
> **Justification** = Its sophisticated package tracking system

Now it's over to you. Follow the formula and start to develop your Positioning Statement. As you work on it use these tips to help you get more clarity around the four questions.

Your target market needs to be:

- Large enough to justify why you're in business.

- Focused enough to allow you to specifically address customer pains.

- Meaningful to the customer – the more strongly customers feel about being part of this group, the better. The more precisely you define the target market, the more members will feel a part of it.

Your frame of reference needs to:

- Include all the options to satisfy a specific, identifiable need.

- Take into account that when your company is positioned as a member of a certain frame of reference, you automatically accrue its benefits as well as its baggage.

Your point of difference needs to be:

- Fact-based – You need to support it with undeniable facts.

- Desirable – It must promise to meet the needs of the customer.

- Pre-emptive – The stronger and longer customers associate your company, and only your company, with this point of difference, the better.

The justification needs to:

- Include unique features, functions, characteristics, or delivery methods

- Be unique and defendable – in other words, bulletproof!

- Keep in mind, your brand promise doesn't have to change the world, it just has to be a promise you can keep and one that hits a chord with your customers.

Brand building examples from Organic Fresh - Positioning

 Brand Foundations

 Our Purpose
(the passion that gets us out of bed everyday!)

**To help people stay healthy for longer
by improving the quality of their food.**

 Our Positioning
(how we position ourselves in the minds of target buyers.)

**For lovers of healthy food, Organic Fresh is the Australian fruit and veg store that provides
highly nutritional 100% pesticide, herbicide and fungicide free produce through our strict
and ethical 'farm to plate' quality control process.**

 Unlock your positioning worksheets here:
http://plan2brand.com/resources/worksheets/
positioningstatement

Step 4

Build the principles that guide your brand

'What does the name Virgin mean? We are a company that likes to take on the giants. In too many businesses, these giants have had things their own way. We are going to have fun competing with them.' – Richard Branson

Step 4: Build the principles that guide your brand

Meet your new best friend – your brand pillars. Your brand pillars are a set of surprisingly powerful key words that embody what your brand is about. Typically your brand pillars are three to five attributes or principles, written as words and supported by a brief description. Your brand pillars should convey the emotional reasons customers will buy from you and they also act as the principles that guide your brand promise.

You should think of them as the non-negotiable attributes or beliefs that stand for who you are and what you do. The best brand pillars address the unmet, or under-met, needs in the market.

For instance, you could argue that the majority of courses and programs available for 'personal training' don't provide enough education around business management. This is possibly an unmet need in the personal training industry. A personal training company could stand apart from its competition by introducing a superior 'business management' unit and adopting 'business education' as a core pillar so they have a needed point of difference to build on.

Brand pillars are critical for helping you develop and manage your brand. Despite what many people think, managing your brand development needn't get complex and consume resources if you have brand pillars and use them as a check against most activities the brand performs.

Your brand pillars are great for keeping your brand consistent. When you're inducting new staff, briefing a web designer, commissioning a brochure or having a sales conversation, you can refer back to your brand pillars for guidance. For example, when you assess a new website proposal you would ask yourself, 'Does this represent the essence behind the words we chose to be our brand pillars?'

Brand pillars will also empower your staff, who will be more confident making decisions when you're not around because they will be clear on the priorities you are focusing on to grow.

Embraced consistently, the unique combination of your three or four values acts as your brand's unique recipe. Think of them as ingredients designed to consolidate your point of difference.

To understand brand pillars better, let's look some notable examples.

Virgin's Brand Pillars

The pillars that Richard Branson has created drive every one of his businesses and when I last checked that was more than 400. At the heart of every company he builds is a clear focus on customer centricity, innovation and his unique vibe. He won't enter into a business unless he can be true to the values outlined by his brand pillars. This is the key to creating the consistent success he has demonstrated since launching Virgin Records in 1973.

Customer centricity	Innovation	Unique vibe
Virgin, no matter what category, will be known for understanding, caring about, fighting for, and delighting the customer. We take customer service very seriously. It's a central brand function, not a side operational function, although it is quite operationalised.	No matter what category we enter – and this takes a bit of discipline because we get opportunities all the time to go into lots of different things – we never want to go in as a 'me too' product. We want to go in and shake things up.	We are cheeky and playful. We constantly innovate, but not at the cost of approachability. We're sort of the CEO in jeans, not taking ourselves too seriously.

Richard could have decided that sustainability took precedence over innovation, which would have led to him creating a completely different style of brand. But he didn't because he has embraced the values he believes in and that he thought mattered to his customers.

Amazon's Brand Pillars

Customer Focus	Frugality	Innovation
"We start with the customer and work backward."	"Amazon is spending money on things that matter to customers."	"I think frugality drives innovation, just like other constraints do."
Following a bottom-up approach, every decision at Amazon is driven by the customers' needs.	Frugality is part of the company's DNA. Amazon is continually looking for ways to do things cost-effectively.	Amazon is always looking for the simple solutions in order to provide lower prices to its customers.

Amazon on the other hand believe their business will be best positioned to beat their competition, appeal to their target market and prosper if they prioritise customer focus, act frugally and innovate at every level. That's how they operate – their three pillars influence every decision any staff member has to make daily.

Dilmah's Brand Pillars

Respect	Ethical	Sustainable
Dilmah is respectful of the traditions of an industry that is centuries old, and of a beverage with a 5,000-year history. The teas they offer are traditional and orthodox made using a process perfected over generations.	Dilmah is an ethical brand, a pioneer in seeking fairness in the world of tea, and benefiting the workers and others in the Ceylon Tea industry through its success.	With the 2010 Declaration of a Core Commitment to Sustainability, Dilmah Conservation is now working towards a more sustainable use of the environment by encouraging a harmonious co-existence between man and nature.

Dilmah demonstrates their uniqueness using completely different pillars. Founded on a passionate commitment to quality and authenticity, the pillars they chose are part philosophy and go beyond commerce. This is what makes Dilmah the first ethically produced tea. Business ethics and social responsibility guide the family business and these values are embodied in their pillars.

How to develop your brand pillars

Your brand can and should reflect your personal style and ambitions, just like Richard Branson. This is how you generate emotional and logical feelings that customers associate with your product or service and why the responsibility of finding your pillars, or values, falls on you.

To find your brand pillars think about the *most important values and characteristics* inherent in business. You won't be able to include *all* your values. It's important that the brand pillars you choose also matter to the Buyer Persona you're targeting.

So before you put pen to paper, spend some time reflecting on the exercises you have already completed.

Looking inside: *Remind yourself of your purpose and think again about what you want to be and why. If you have an operating history, what stories or culture could make for potential brand ingredients?*

Looking outside: *Think about your customers, your competitors and the market, then ask yourself what financial, emotional, physical or spiritual benefits your products or services provide your customer. What needs or desires do they satisfy?*

Compared to the competition, what makes your company unique?

Where is your industry or market going? Is there a way you can take advantage of these changes?

Following is a process to guide you as you begin thinking about your possible brand pillars. Keep in mind that something as grounding and important as your pillars, the principals that will set the standards of your brand and hold you to account on a daily level, can take some deep thinking to resolve.

Step 1: Look at the following list compiled from a number of the world's greatest brands. Use it as a starting point only as you begin to think about the pillars (think values) that could drive your brand.

Community	Teamwork	Comfort	Integrity
Nurturing	Family	Ethical	Knowledge
Innovation	Competitiveness	Health	Quality
Value	Entertainment	Responsiveness	Cleanliness
Diversity	Connection	Education	Fairness
Reliability	Authenticity	Pragmatism	Security
Trust	Commitment	People	Honesty
Positive	Disclosure	Sense of	Advanced
outlook	Fun	urgency	technology
Irreverence	Performance	Precision	Growth
Underpromise,	Simplicity	Safety	Customer focus
overdeliver		Affordability	Creativity
			Accountability
			Variety

Step 2: Write down six to eight potential brand pillars using the list above or any other values your feel strongly about.

Step 3: Use the following questions to make sure that the pillars you end up with are core pillars. Think about:

- Which of the words listed above are so part of your DNA that, if they disappeared, your company would cease to exist as it is?

- Which ones do you believe your company can adhere to in the face of all obstacles?

- Which ones are you very passionate about?

- Which ones do you feel are inherently part of you and reflect the way you naturally approach things?

Step 4: Now choose three pillars that you believe are core to your company, and write a one or two sentence explanation of what that pillar means to you and your business and how you will live it through your brand.

Brand building examples from Organic Fresh - Pillars

Brand Foundations

Our Purpose
(the passion that gets us out of bed everyday!)

To help people stay healthy for longer by improving the quality of their food.

Our Positioning
(how we position ourselves in the minds of target buyers.)

For lovers of healthy food, Organic Fresh is the Australian fruit and veg store that provides highly nutritional 100% pesticide, herbicide and fungicide free produce through our strict and ethical 'farm to plate' quality control process.

Our Pillars
(attributes/principles that we stand by, no matter what)

Exceptional quality	Chemical Free	Grown in Australia
We only purchase directly from farmers, bypassing all intermediaries.	We ensure all of our products are certified free from common, pesticides, herbicides and fungicides.	Many competitors source produce from overseas.
This gives us the edge in ensuring all products meet our strict standards for quality, nutrition and freshness.	We only process them in our own facilities to guarantee purity.	To guarantee fresh and nutrient rich produce we only buy from local farms. Grown in Australia is an important market differentiator.

Unlock your brand pillar worksheets here: http://plan2brand.com/resources/worksheets/ brandpillars

Step  5

Create your promise

'Logos and branding are so important. In a big part of the world, people cannot read French or English, but are great in remembering signs.'
– Karl Lagerfeld

Step 5: Create your promise

The next piece of the 'brand jigsaw' is your brand promise – a high overarching statement that you make to customers that identifies what they should expect from all interactions with your staff, products, services and company. It is often associated with the company name and/or logo.

In a nutshell, it's the shortest and simplest way to tell the world what you do and the value you deliver. It drives many internal aspects of your business and also informs your marketing. It represents everything a company stands for, and when you nail it, it goes beyond the rational benefits that managed to attract customers in the past and extols a higher-order emotional reward.

A brand Promise:

- Is not a slogan, or advertising headline.

- Is not, by definition, a public statement (though it can be as long as your brand truly lives up to it).

These three invented examples get the point across well.

For a heating and air conditioning company:

ABC Heating and Air -- "We're not comfortable until you are."

For a tire company:

Dave's Tire Company -- "More than tires, we deliver peace of mind."

For a fine dining restaurant:

Carl's Steak House -- "Our food is the best, but the memories we help you create are even better."

Virgin's is a good example. Their brand promise is:

"To be the consumer champion while being genuine, fun, contemporary and different in everything we do at a reasonable price."

Empowered customers are shaping business today

Today's customers want immediate value and will go elsewhere if you can't provide it, and a purposeful brand promise plays an important role in communicating the value you offer.

A strong brand promise:

- Drives new attitudes and behaviors across your team.

- Evolves your marketing and advertising.

- Inspires new product development.

- Makes your workplace more humane, more respectful, and more productive.

Brand promise and the consumer

As marketers we take brand promises for granted. We just accept that every brand in its right mind has one and that it is committed to keeping it. As consumers, we have no such awareness. We don't wander around with the promises of our favorite brands on our devices checking that, wherever we see them, they are doing what they said they would do in the promise.

In fact, ask any consumer to articulate the promise of their favorite brand and all will struggle. What does Google promise? I don't know exactly. What is the exact wording of the Moleskine promise? I have no idea. I think Starbucks promises me great coffee, but again I'm not 100% positive.

What we do have are impressions – perceptions accumulated from all our encounters with the brands we come across each day that tell us what we think we can expect. In all likelihood we subconsciously interpret those as a promise.

Four expectations that matter to your customer

These impressions, and the promise they amount to give us a set of expectations. Let's now look in a little more detail at how this works. Expectations around a brand are informed by four broad categories.

1) The first category is **sector**. Your brand is part of a sector that makes specific promises in the mind of the consumer. Examples include:

   - We expect fresh food at a supermarket.

   - We expect a taxi to be safe.

   - We expect a fashion brand to be energetic and full of ideas.

   - We expect our Internet to be fast.

   - We expect the trains to run and the planes to fly.

   But meeting all these 'sector' expectations gives a brand nothing beyond participation. It doesn't make you exceptional in any way.

2) The second category is **price.** This also gives consumers expectations. We look for higher-priced products to deliver greater quality, reliability and comfort. We expect to get what we pay for. But unless you are talking about conspicuous consumption luxury products, price alone is not the basis for a compelling promise.

3) Thirdly, marketers talk about **service** expectations at length and about the need for brands to exceed customer expectations in order to succeed. They take their cues for this from customers who, not surprisingly, when asked what else they would like, quickly look to collectively raise the returns. I call this the 'Gimme' deception. Asked what they would like, customers say 'gimme more'. They want:

- More personnalisation

- More options

- More attention

- Faster service

- Shorter processes

But while consumers punish bad service, that doesn't mean the inverse dynamic applies. It has been found that 'delighting customers doesn't build loyalty; reducing their effort—the work they must do to get their problem solved—does.'

So simply giving the customers more is not the basis for a brand promise.

4) This brings us to the fourth category, the big one – **brand**. The style and nature of a brand, its personality, has a significant impact on consumer expectations. In fact, I believe a brand's character is the most powerful factor influencing a consumer's expectations, and therefore what it should promise. A brand promise:

- Helps consumers decide what the brand is capable of.

- Creates interpersonal experiences by telegraphing to consumers how they can expect the brand to relate to them.

- Helps consumers decide how much they can rely on the brand to do good by them.

Given that sector and service expectations for the most part are non-differentiating, and that price reflects, but doesn't make the promise, how a brand chooses to behave decides what it gets to promise, not the other way round.

It's about feelings

A brand promise is not about what consumers get; it's about what consumers get to feel. Until consumers get a feeling that they'd like to get again and again, that they don't/can't get anywhere else, you haven't promised them anything great at all. You don't promise and then deliver.

You have to deliver first, and that becomes the promise.

As you begin to think about creating your brand promise, the starting point is thinking about your customer's needs and how your product or service intends to be different in the marketplace while addressing those needs. Whatever the customer needs, you must be able to demonstrate how you provide it better and can offer a higher level of customer satisfaction than the competition. This is why having a point of difference is so critical.

The construct of a brand promise you can use a simple formula that connects you and your community.

What You Do and for Whom.

This takes the bold catchiness from the tagline school of thought and reinforces it with the essence of the mission. And while you can wordsmith it all you want, most of us can fill in the blanks of this very basic formula.

Take our brand promise, for example.

"Strategic planning, goal setting, and brand building made easy for SME's."

It immediately tells you what we do, but it also guides many daily decisions we make. It's one of the reasons I wrote this book. It's the reason we have moved from building websites for clients to conducting workshops and creating an online platform that educates as many people as possible about strategic branding.

Your brand promise doesn't necessarily need to be customer facing. For example, Nike has had many customer facing slogans including the iconic 'Just Do It'. However, these phrases have been marketing tag-lines as opposed to their brand promise, which is, 'to bring inspiration and innovation to every athlete* in the world'. The asterisk then goes on to note that 'If you have a body, you're an athlete.'

What makes a brand promise 'deliver' is that it is unique and makes you different from the competition. Because if you can't clearly define what differentiates you from the competition and a reason that potential customers should buy from you rather than the competition, you are most likely in a commodity situation and susceptible to price shopping.

Case study

In my line of work I'm fortunate enough to have discussions with various business owners who open up to me, often talking about their fears and failings. One CEO I respect enormously managed to go from start-up to over 500 employees in the space of just over three years. His company produces high quality products in the technology sector and despite its rapid growth and obvious success, the CEO was then very concerned about maintaining his trajectory.

He admitted to me that to get to where he was he had been micromanaging the company and sometimes winging it by doing things such as selecting his staff on a gut feel. It was apparent to him that his business growth was the result of a little bit of luck, intuition, trial and error and liberal doses of agility. Sound familiar? He was now asking himself if his management style was sustainable or suitable to take his business to the next level. You can guess the answer.

He confided in me that the company was starting to experience growing employee turnover through job dissatisfaction and for the first time felt challenged with managing the future.

The root of the company's problem came from never formally articulating its purpose, vision or pillars – all covered in the previous steps. The point is that without these the business was not able to craft its brand promise – their core selling idea – the shortest and simplest way to demonstrate to their prospects, customers, staff and stakeholders exactly what they were delivering and the value that differentiates them.

This meant that the employees that were not working closely with the CEO weren't quite sure what the company's broader aims were. They felt powerless to influence or contribute positively to the company because they weren't clear on the company's higher purpose and what role they could play in contributing to the larger vision. For them, they simply had a job.

We discussed how purpose, vision, pillars and brand promises were not just a collection of words but also a strategic collection of words that bring into existence a shared vision that motivates people to support a cause and mobilises them around what they can contribute to see the company succeed.

If you're trying to be all things to all people in your daily struggle to stay afloat, it's hard to achieve even the first point. My most powerful advice for achieving meaningful differentiation is to never use your competition as a benchmark. Make the competition irrelevant and challenge the status quo. Just because 'we've always done it that way' doesn't mean you have to keep doing it that way.

Remember, your brand promise is at the heart of an effective strategy to differentiate your firm from the competition. And your devotion to delivering on the promise must be maniacal and complete or the promise becomes an empty slogan.

 Unlock your brand promise worksheet here: http://plan2brand.com/resources/worksheets/ brandpromise

Brand building examples from Organic Fresh – Promise

Brand Foundations

Our Purpose
(the passion that gets us out of bed everyday!)

To help people stay healthy for longer by improving the quality of their food.

Our Positioning
(how we position ourselves in the minds of target buyers.)

For lovers of healthy food, Organic Fresh is the Australian fruit and veg store that provides highly nutritional 100% pesticide, herbicide and fungicide free produce through our strict and ethical 'farm to plate' quality control process.

Our Pillars
(attributes/principles that we stand by, no matter what)

Exceptional quality	Chemical Free	Grown in Australia
We only purchase directly from farmers, bypassing all intermediaries.	We ensure all of our products are certified free from common, pesticides, herbicides and fungicides.	Many competitors source produce from overseas.
This gives us the edge in ensuring all products meet our strict standards for quality, nutrition and freshness.	We only process them in our own facilities to guarantee purity.	To guarantee fresh and nutrient rich produce we only buy from local farms. Grown in Australia is an important market differentiator.

Our Promise
(Connecting Purpose, Pillars, and Positioning to deliver an emotionally connected and differentiated customer experience.)

Feel healthy, have energy – everyday.

Get fresh and tasty 100% chemical free organic produce from locally sourced Australian farms.

Promise Dimensions
(The three most important aspects including objectives and activities to consistently deliver and bring your Promise 'to life' for customers.)

Fresh and tasty organics

Which means

Customers experience superior quality and fresh taste every time.

Each store's display is always beautifully presented and staff take every care to minimise perishable nature of products.

Reassurance of ethical standards from customers knowing who suppliers are and how they produce the food they eat.

Touchpoint action
- Staff Induction Manual
- Presentation/storage training
- 'Farm to Plate' reporting
- Machinery calibration
- Monthly supplier meetings
- 'Meet supplier' in store
- Test & Measure procedures

Inspirational organic knowledge

Which means

Customers find a wealth of interesting and informative content about our local suppliers, our processes and organics health benefits, in store and online.

We are knowledgable and love to answer questions and advise our customers.

We embrace the organic way and help our customers revitalise eating habits.

Touchpoint action
- Point of sale information
- Instore organic library/recipes
- Blog, ePapers/Whitepapers
- Staff training on trends, facts, misnomers
- Nuture partnerships

Easy access to organics

Which means

Customers get 100% fresh, organic and food delivered 7 days a week in all major capitals in Australia through online store.

Touchpoint action
- Website store
- Delivery van graphics
- Recycle/return boxes
- Loyalty Program

Step 6

Clarify your vision

As the Cheshire cat famously said: 'If you don't know where you're going, it doesn't matter which way you go.' – Alice in Wonderland

Step 6: Clarify your vision

Arguably the most visionary business leader who lived in our lifetime was Steve Jobs. In late 2012 a full-length version of a 'lost' Steve Jobs speech given at a Design Conference in Aspen, in 1983, was unearthed and posted on the web. Here is a link to it – http://bit.ly/1Didvxn.

The highlight of this thirty-year-old recording is during the question and answer session. Steve describes mobile computing, something nobody had envisioned up until then, pointing out that he would like to one-day build a computer in a slate-like form. He was describing *today's iPad* twenty-five years before its creation. Looking back now we all see how Steve's expansive vision helped build one of the most game changing brands of this century.

If you run an organisation, no matter how big or small, you have a lot riding on the success of that business. If I asked you, could you clearly tell me where your business is going in the next year? What about the next five years? What does the future look like? Are you driven, focused and committed, and is your staff enthusiastic and fired up by your vision?

Or are you are simply reacting to daily forces instead and barely following a plan of any kind?

Running a business is a big job, and the biggest challenge is to succeed. So what can you do to move forward, create positive change, reinvigorate yourself and your staff, and where should you start? If you define your future, you will be able to see the path more clearly. That's the role of your brand's vision.

What is a vision?

A vision, quite simply, is a picture of what success will be at a particular time in the future. It's about what you want to become, and along with your purpose, it is the overarching drive for your business.

> The 'golden rule' when crafting the Vision Statement is: It should require great effort to create, but should not require great effort to understand.

Without a vision of where you're going how can you develop a plan to get there, and how will you know when you've arrived?

Without one, you're left pushing through business challenges each day, climbing mountain after mountain, only to discover each time you arrive somewhere that is not really where you want to be. Nothing was ever created without a vision. It gives us direction and purpose and can serve as a powerful motivator for those around us and ourselves.

In order to truly guide and motivate, a vision must:

- Be aligned with the core values of both you and your business.

- Be effectively communicated to, and accepted by, everyone involved in the company.

The more precise and detailed you are in writing a description of your vision of the future, the easier it will be to communicate it to others and gain their commitment to it, and the more likely you will be to achieve it.

Success comes through bringing people on board such as partners, employees or consultants – who have similar core values to you. People who understand and accept the business vision as matching closely with their own ideals will help you achieve what you want faster.

Developing a vision that is truly shared takes time, effort, energy and commitment. You can't expect that, just because you develop a vision statement, read them at a staff meeting and even hand them out in printed form, everyone will immediately accept and work toward achieving them. You need to walk the talk and be totally committed to your vision first, and then discuss it with your employees and consultants at least eight or ten times before they will believe you're really serious.

What are the benefits of having an effective vision?

The benefits of sharing your vision are many and varied. Here are just a few:

- It acts as a unifying force for everyone in your business to align and focus efforts on your goal.

- It guides everyone's decision making and planning.

- It acts as a barometer for your business strategy.

- It can motivate and inspire everyone to commit to a communal goal.

- It guides the type of people you will employ.

- It reflects, and can help to define, your core values and beliefs.

- It can be the guiding light in times of change.

> Above all, your vision should be a seductive image of the ideal future.

What does a vision statement look like?

Vision statements come in many forms; they can be as long or as short as you like. It's your vision so I'm not about to dictate how many words it should be. I've seen some that go over a page in length. Let's look at a few.

Many household businesses only have one-line vision statements.

Mary Kay: *To give unlimited opportunity to women.*

Walt Disney: *To make people happy.*

Ford: *To become the world's leading consumer company for automotive products and services.*

While some entrepreneurs take the 'less is better' tactic, others prefer to flesh out their vision statement with a few more sentences and include clear-cut goals and expectations for the organisation.

Citigroup: *Our goal for Citigroup is to be the most respected global financial services company. Like any other public company, we're obligated to deliver profits and growth to our shareholders. Of equal importance is to deliver those profits and generate growth responsibly.*

The Estee Lauder Company: *The guiding vision of The Estee Lauder Company is 'Bringing the best to everyone we touch.' By 'the best,' we mean the best products, the best people and the best ideas. These three pillars have been the hallmarks of our company since Mrs Estee Lauder founded it in 1946. They remain the foundation upon which we continue to build our success today.*

Heinz: *The world's premier food company, offering nutritious, superior tasting foods to people everywhere. Being the premier food company does not mean being the biggest, but does mean being the best in terms of consumer value, customer service, employee talent, and consistent and predictable growth.*

Are you ready to write yours?

If you don't already have a vision statement, creating one is your next step.

Looking at the previous vision statement examples should give you a good jumping off point for knowing what a vision statement is. As a guide remember:

- The best corporate or company vision statements are brief and succinct (yes, I know I said you could make it any length); it will say a lot in just a few words, so those words must be very carefully chosen.

- The key to a good vision statement is to think of things in a long-term, broad sense, without sounding generic.

- If you're too specific, you will limit your vision and it won't be applicable ten years down the road. For example, if your current goal for your business is to move into a larger building, that's a vision for the future but it's not the vision for the future of your entire business. It's too narrow in focus.

- On the other hand, if you say that you want to achieve success – well, any business in the world could say that. It's too generic. The best statement will be clear about what success looks like.

Your vision is your goal or goals, and being able to state them clearly is the first step toward making them happen.

Unlike business plans, vision statements generally don't outline a plan to achieve those goals. But by outlining the key objectives for a company, they enable your employees to develop business strategies to achieve the stated goals.

Writing a good vision statement is straightforward for some, and can be challenging for others. Think about what your business does and what, in an ideal world, you would like it to do and how you would like to appear to the outside world. Consider the services and attributes that your company provides, then imagine how it would be if you provided the very best version of them possible. List those visions, and incorporate them into a brief statement that gives a good overview of the kind of image you want to represent.

Then put them aside. Ruminate. Take some time to talk with friends and peers. Google vision statements and do some of your own research. Look at companies you admire, both in your industry and outside your industry.

 Unlock your vision worksheet here: http:// plan2brand.com/resources/worksheets/ visionbrandpromise

Case study

Warby Parker is an American brand of prescription eyeglasses and sunglasses founded in 2010. Warby Parker sells online and has a limited number of showrooms in the United States.

Warby Parker have a very simple and clear vision: to "create boutique-quality, classically crafted eyewear at a revolutionary price point."

By designing glasses in-house and selling only directly to consumers, the company lowers the cost of its glasses by a significant amount. At the time we went to print their glasses retailed at around US$95 - to put this in perspective, the National Association of Vision Care Plans has stated that the average price of eyeglasses is US$263.

To understand where their vision came from they explain on their website:

"Every idea starts with a problem. Ours was simple: glasses are too expensive. We were students when one of us lost his glasses on a backpacking trip. The cost of replacing them was so high that he spent the first semester of grad school without them, squinting and complaining. (We don't recommend this.) The rest of us had similar experiences, and we were amazed at how hard it was to find a pair of great frames that didn't leave our wallets bare. Where were the options?

It turns out there was a simple explanation. The eyewear industry is dominated by a single company that has been able to keep prices artificially high while reaping huge profits from consumers who have no other options.

We started Warby Parker to create an alternative."

In just five years Warby Parker have pulled off the impossible — selling something as personal and vital to your everyday wellbeing as eyeglasses completely online. Since they graced the pages of GQ being labeled "the Netflix of eyewear" earlier this year, the eyewear brand has exploded.

Brand building examples from Organic Fresh – Vision

Brand Foundations

Our Purpose
(the passion that gets us out of bed everyday!)

To help people stay healthy for longer by improving the quality of their food.

Our Vision
(where we want to be, our future goal)

To be recognised as the No. 1 organic food store in Australia by 2020.

Our Positioning
(how we position ourselves in the minds of target buyers.)

For lovers of healthy food, Organic Fresh is the Australian fruit and veg store that provides highly nutritional 100% pesticide, herbicide and fungicide free produce through our strict and ethical 'farm to plate' quality control process.

Our Pillars
(attributes/principles that we stand by, no matter what)

Exceptional quality

We only purchase directly from farmers, bypassing all intermediaries.

This gives us the edge in ensuring all products meet our strict standards for quality, nutrition and freshness.

Chemical Free

We ensure all of our products are certified free from common, pesticides, herbicides and fungicides.

We only process them in our own facilities to guarantee purity.

Grown in Australia

Many competitors source produce from overseas.

To guarantee fresh and nutrient rich produce we only buy from local farms. Grown in Australia is an important market differentiator.

Our Promise
(Connecting Purpose, Pillars, and Positioning to deliver an emotionally connected and differentiated customer experience.)

Feel healthy, have energy – everyday.

Get fresh and tasty 100% chemical free organic produce from locally sourced Australian farms.

Promise Dimensions
(The three most important aspects including objectives and activities to consistently deliver and bring your Promise 'to life' for customers.)

Fresh and tasty organics

Which means

Customers experience superior quality and fresh taste every time.

Each store's display is always beautifully presented and staff take every care to minimise perishable nature of products.

Reassurance of ethical standards from customers knowing who suppliers are and how they produce the food they eat.

Touchpoint action

- Staff Induction Manual
- Presentation/storage training
- 'Farm to Plate' reporting
- Machinery calibration
- Monthly supplier meetings
- 'Meet supplier' in store
- Test & Measure procedures

Inspirational organic knowledge

Which means

Customers find a wealth of interesting and informative content about our local suppliers, our processes and organics health benefits, in store and online.

We are knowledgable and love to answer questions and advise our customers.

We embrace the organic way and help our customers revitalise eating habits.

Touchpoint action

- Point of sale information
- Instore organic library/recipes
- Blog, ePapers/Whitepapers
- Staff training on trends, facts, misnomers
- Nuture partnerships

Easy access to organics

Which means

Customers get 100% fresh, organic and food delivered 7 days a week in all major capitals in Australia through online store.

Touchpoint action

- Website store
- Delivery van graphics
- Recycle/return boxes
- Loyalty Program

Step 7

Show them you're human

"Be yourself. Everyone else is taken."
– Oscar Wilde

Step 7: Show them you're human

By now you can see that a large part of any brand strategy is inward facing and guides many business decisions. Now that you've worked through six of the seven steps that make up your brand's foundations, it's time to decide how to express your brand's purpose, vision, and the values represented by your pillars, through your brand personality.

This is the bridge that connects your company's internal essence to the external customer experience you want to deliver.

And there's very good reasons to do it...

Quite frankly, human behavior can be baffling. While price, efficiency, and convenience are assumed to be important when it comes to selecting a product or service, don't bet on it every time. Your prospects will sometimes covet products or services that aren't logically the best fit but appeal to them on an emotional level. This attachment can take their relationship with a brand beyond a mere marriage of convenience, to the meeting of soul mates.

Why personality makes a difference

A strong personality plays an important role in differentiating a brand's products or services, particularly in globally competitive markets.

It has long been accepted that customers do not opt for products based on their features alone, they also base their choices on symbolic worth. We all gravitate to, and warm to, certain people because of their personality, and it's no different with brands. Just as your personality is unique to you, your brand's personality should also be unique.

When a customer identifies with the personality of a brand, it can mimic the connection between people. This promotes trust, encourages brand loyalty, and makes a brand memorable. The willingness of Apple fans to wait patiently for upgrades, forgive Apple its flaws, and defend the company against detractors is a demonstration of their strong relationship with the brand.

The reality is branding has almost nothing to do with a lot of the things bankers obsess over — annual percentage rates, product features/functions, money, numbers and spreadsheets. Branding is about people's emotions. Feelings. You can't possibly begin to utilize your organization's brand if you don't understand its underlying emotional associations.

By exploring your brand's personality, you shift the conversation away from left-brained banker speak and into the emotional, right-brained world of consumer perceptions and feelings.

What is brand personality?

Our personalities are a mysterious force that attracts us to certain individuals and repels us from others. Consumers today stretch that concept beyond purely human relationships to their dealings with services and merchandise.

Customers often use terms to define brand personalities that seem to go beyond the psychological definition of personality and involve gender, age, or socioeconomic status. For instance, when describing Harley Davidson, customers use terms like 'bold' and 'empowering.' However, terms like *bold* may be shorthand for conventional personality traits like *aggressiveness* or *ruggedness*.

Descriptors that are relevant to personality invariably indicate the perception of how a brand typically thinks and behaves – *its character.*

You're not always in good company

It would be nice to think that a product or service's brand personality is thought of positively. But this is not always the case. For instance, brands that individuals claim haven't any personality are most often related to dominant telcos or banks. When asked to explain these corporations as an individual, customers often provide vivid, though mostly negative descriptors like dull, greedy and faceless. Therefore perceived lack of brand personality typically suggests an unattractive or weak personality.

> 'A brand personality is the unique, authentic, and talkable soul of your brand that people can get passionate about.'
> – Rohit Bhargay

Know the target market

The attractiveness of a brand's personality relies upon its customers' personalities. Customers are attracted to brands that align with their self-image. This is why in step 3, your buyer persona, we focused on gaining an intimate understanding of your ideal prospects behaviors, needs and goals.

One size doesn't fit all

SME's are at a great advantage when it comes to maintaining a positive brand personality. Driven by shareholders expectations and the need for every increasing market share and profit, dominant market players can often struggle. They can fall into the trap of starting to appeal to everyone.

Starbucks had a strong personality, but since it has expanded worldwide it has become faceless. When Starbucks first opened a coffee house in 1984 it was a challenger within the market. It offered European-style coffee houses unique in the U.S. market and focused on quality, freshness, and an individual experience. In Starbucks' global domination that followed in 1999, the individuality and brand believability weakened.

According to Howard Schultz, founder of Starbucks, 'The key threat to the Starbucks brand was a growing belief among customers that the company was becoming corporate, predictable, inaccessible or irrelevant.'

To yourself be true

A strong brand personality begins with authentic brand values. This is where you should look back and review your brand pillars because these will set you on the path to defining your brand's personality.

As discussed in step 5, your pillars should permeate through your organization, therefore affecting policies, attitudes of employees, and also the company's culture.

A good example is in Google's company philosophy: 'You can make money without doing evil.' This value initially directed the organization to form choices centered on its customers' needs, not on profit alone. Values should be proven in company behavior or public trust will be eroded. As Google continues to grow, you wouldn't be the only one thinking that they are no longer living true to some of their original values.

Communicate consistently

Customers' trust in a brand's personality depends on the consistency with which it is communicated across all the touch points they interact with. It's important to ensure there's alignment with the visual aspects of your product or service, as well as the written and oral communications.

There is a misconception that your brand personality is the responsibility of the designer who decides how the brand will look and that the colours and pictures used in a website or brochure make up the sum total of a brand's personality. Just like your personality, a brand personality is expressed in everything your company says and does, not just the way it looks.

Every time customers read something on a company's website or chat with its employees, they make judgments about its brand personality based on tone of voice. If an individual keeps changing his tone of voice radically with every interaction, one is inclined to trust him less. The same is true for brands. To be credible and appear authentic to customers, the company's tone of voice must sound human and be consistent.

Imagine a tax consultant whose purpose is to eliminate the stress his clients associate with taxation and compliance. Every aspect of his business personality should reflect honesty, compassion and calmness. From the subject and the tone of voice in the blog articles he writes through to a helpful website that offers plenty of free advice.

But more than publishing articles on your blog or writing and designing your website, your brand personality should permeate throughout your entire organisation, no matter how large or small.

How far do some brands go?

There are plenty of brands I could highlight to show you brand personality in action. Just one example is an American brand called Moosejaw, a retailer and e-commerce store specialising in outdoor recreation apparel and equipment. Moosejaw successfully differentiates themselves from their competitors by demonstrating a hilarious and quirky personality that runs through all of its website copy, advertising and customer service channels.

Moosejaw's personality is irreverent, edgy and playful.

Here are some examples of copy from their website that reinforce their personality:

- 'You don't need to be a certified badass to wear this stuff.'

- 'What's new: We just added this stuff like five minutes ago. That may not be true but it sure sounds good.'

- 'The best stuff: We're pretty sure this is the best stuff. Or at least decent stuff.'

Here is an example of an email that reinforces their playful personality. This was sent to an online buyer after their purchase was dispatched.

Thanks for your order with 1-Day! Invoice # 1367087

Your product has been painstakingly removed from our shelves, the dust wiped free, and carefully placed inside its packaging. It has gone through a number of checks and all with contamination free sterilised gloves.

A hush echoed through the 100 staff as the final tape locked down the packaging. We all linked arms and swayed in time (except for Luke who was swinging his hips in the opposite direction to everyone else) and sung the 1-day version of 'I'm leaving.... On a jet plane'. Real tears were shed by some of us, who are still coming to terms with the fact the product has left the building for good.

If the suspense is too much you can also track your order's location in transit using the following details to view the package status:

Courier Company : Courier Post
Tracking Number : OC105344178NZ
Website :
http://www.trackandtrace.courierpost.co.nz/search/OC105344178NZ

If it's not showing straight away don't panic, it'll just be that we've been so keen to let you know your bargain is on its way that the Courier Company haven't had a chance to update their system yet.

We trust you have enjoyed your 1-day shopping experience and know that your package will be with you very soon. Check out tomorrow's deals at 12pm - we'll start working on Luke's rhythm, while we wait to see you again soon

Thanks heaps from the team @ 1-day.

Think about how a defined personality could influence how your staff answers your phones, what your email signature says or the experience customers have when visiting your premises.

Let Carl Jung guide the way

There are dozens of exercises you can explore to build out your brand personality. Possibly the best overarching exercise you can consider is deciding which Archetype best represents the brand you want to build. Following is a description of the 12 Archetypes conceived by famed Swiss psychologist, Carl Jung, more than half a century ago.

How Archetypes influence your brand personality

Jung's 12 Archetypes are universally accepted as the core characters that provide emotional prompts to fundamental human desires. The idea behind using brand archetypes to define your brand personality is to anchor your brand against something iconic—something already embedded within the conscious and subconscious of humanity. Aligning your brand with a brand archetype makes your brand easier to identify and will help you to define what personality will suit your brand.

These archetypes are so remarkable because they tap into specific core desires, drives, fears and motivations all humans have. They can help you understand who your brand is and what it stands for. Especially for 'me too' categories and commodity businesses, archetypes reveal unique differentiators and meaning beyond what a company sells.

To start this process, you need to identify the primary brand archetype or brand personality from the descriptions of Jung's list of 12 below. See if you can decide which applies to you or your organization. You may feel that your brand is a combination of archetypes. This is not uncommon. Do your best to isolate one by looking back at your purpose, vision and pillars.

The 12 archetypes are:

1. **The Caregiver** brand

   The Caregiver **brand** is moved by compassion, generosity and selflessness to help and serve others. Caregiver cultures are responsive, consistent, and trustworthy. They're strongest when they are acting as a mentor for employees or clients.

   Examples include Campbell's, Johnson & Johnson and TOMS shoes, Dove, Amnesty International and insurance companies.

2. The Every Person brand

   The Every Person brand believes in the inherent worth and dignity of all, expecting very little from life but committed to teaching through empathy, realism and street smarts. Every person cultures often revolve around committee or support groups where people of all levels bond together to collaborate.

   Examples include Gap, Habitat for Humanity, Levis, Target and Ikea.

3. The Hero brand

   The Hero brand is tough and courageous, overcomes tremendous obstacles and persists in difficult times. They are most fulfilled when they can rise to or overcome a challenge. Hero cultures are highly productive, disciplined, and focused. They're the champions of courage, inspiring us all to be a little braver.

Examples include Nike, Robert Irvine, PayPal, Doctors Without Borders, Duracell.

4. The Innocent brand

    The Innocent brand is a spontaneous, trusting child who always sees the bright side of a situation and is able to maintain an optimistic, spontaneous, trusting outlook. Innocents are the exemplars of optimism. Through simple acts of kindness or a trusting smile, they are consistent and unpretentious.

    Examples include Avon, Hello Kitty, Tumblr and Coca-Cola.

5. The Explorer brand

    The Explorer brand moves past the known to explore new, uncharted territories. When crowds go one way, explorers choose a completely different path, embracing the journey rather than the destination. Explorer cultures are determined to get us to step out of life and into living. Independent, self-directed, and at the forefront of theory and practice, they're inherently non-conformist.

    Examples include The North Face, Subaru, Patagonia, Starbucks, NASA, the Boy Scouts, National Geographic.

6. The Rebel brand

    The Rebel brand embodies rage about structures that no longer serve, even when these structures are supported by societies and our conscious choices. Rebels are rule breakers and catalysts for change. Rebels stand up for what they believe in so we can all break away from what's conventional.

    Examples include Harley Davidson, Virgin, Diesel, Greenpeace, E*TRADE, Uber, Netflix.

7. **The Lover brand**

   The Lover brand lives to experience pleasure, achieve intimacy and follow bliss. Their ability to tap into a multi-dimensional experience is commonly carried throughout the retail, hospitality, tourism and entertainment industries with fans of all varieties.

   Examples include Victoria's Secret, BMW, Moët & Chandon, eHarmony, Tiffany & Co. and Häagen-Dazs.

8. The Creator brand

   The Creator brand fosters imaginative endeavors, aiming to express and turn away from mediocrity. Of every music note possible, they combine just the right ones in harmony. Of every word, every mechanical piece, they find fluidity and order. They trust the creative process because they have the imagination to see it through.

   Examples include HGTV, Canon, Adobe, LEGO, Pixar, Warner Music, Pinterest, Shutterstock.

9. The Jester brand

   The Jester brand lives to have a good time, making the most mundane experiences something fun. Innovative and outspoken, Jesters are the first to suggest a cocktail after a hard day. Their fun-loving attitudes make people say, "Hey, I want to hang out with them!" As a service provider, they help us all take the pain out of life's hardest moments.

   Examples include GEICO, Taco Bell, Skittles, MailChimp, Ben & Jerry's, Moosejaw, Southwest Airlines.

10. The Sage brand

    The Sage brand seeks the truths that will set us free in seeing the world objectively and providing course-corrective solutions based on objective analysis of our actions and choices. They will always bring a well thought-out method to the table and you can guarantee they'll be able to prove their results.

    Examples include CNN, Oprah, The Wall Street Journal, The Smithsonian, Mayo Clinic, Rosetta Stone, and Harvard.

11. The Magician brand

    The Magician brand seeks out the fundamental laws of science and metaphysics to understand how to transform situations, influence people, and transform visions into reality. At a Magician organization, impossible is only a state of mind. The Magician often finds its way into a consultancy, training, or coaching organization as they help clients change their outlooks on life.

    Examples include TED, Disney, MAC Cosmetics, Polaroid, Apple, and Dyson.

12. The Ruler brand

    The Ruler brand inspires us to take responsibility for our own lives in our society and in the world at large by creating environments that invite gifts and perspectives of all concerned. They resolve complex problems and protect the world from chaos. Rulers are also experts at balancing multiple stakeholders and displaying exceptional leadership qualities.

    Examples include Mercedes-Benz, British Airways, Rolex, Rolls Royce and American Express.

Understanding your brand's archetype

Understanding which archetype your brand should live out will enable you to define its personality and the role you want your brand to play in people's lives and the story you want to tell about who you are and what you stand for.

As humans, the fact is that we're drawn to all of these archetypes, and we see a bit of ourselves expressed across multiple dimensions and personalities. The earlier on in your company's journey that you can uncover your brand's personality, the sooner your team can begin living it and you can build on it. Then you will find it easier to leave a consistent lasting impression in your audience's minds, regardless of whether you're running a small business or big company.

A small business that can develop a recognisable brand personality will have a much better chance of success. Consider all of the ways you can inject your personality into every aspect of your branding strategy. If you do, people will remember you the next time they're looking for what you have to offer.

 For more help unlock the brand personality worksheets here: http://plan2brand.com/ resources/worksheets/brandpersonality

Based on Organic Fresh's archetype, 'Sage', we developed the following brand personality. This completes their brand Foundations.

Brand Foundations

Our Purpose
(the passion that gets us out of bed everyday!)

To help people stay healthy for longer by improving the quality of their food.

Our Vision
(where we want to be, our future goal)

To be recognised as the No. 1 organic food store in Australia by 2020.

Our Positioning
(how we position ourselves in the minds of target buyers.)

For lovers of healthy food, Organic Fresh is the Australian fruit and veg store that provides highly nutritional 100% pesticide, herbicide and fungicide free produce through our strict and ethical 'farm to plate' quality control process.

Our Pillars
(attributes/principles that we stand by, no matter what)

Exceptional quality

We only purchase directly from farmers, bypassing all intermediaries.

This gives us the edge in ensuring all products meet our strict standards for quality, nutrition and freshness.

Chemical Free

We ensure all of our products are certified free from common, pesticides, herbicides and fungicides.

We only process them in our own facilities to guarantee purity.

Grown in Australia

Many competitors source produce from overseas.

To guarantee fresh and nutrient rich produce we only buy from local farms. Grown in Australia is an important market differentiator.

Our Promise
(Connecting Purpose, Pillars, and Positioning to deliver an emotionally connected and differentiated customer experience.)

Feel healthy, have energy – everyday.

Get fresh and tasty 100% chemical free organic produce from locally sourced Australian farms.

Our Personality
(Human characteristics/traits that define how we speak and behave, to connect emotionally with our target market.)

Outspoken
Does mean

We are single-minded in our belief in Organics. We are frank, straightforward, tell it like it is.

Doesn't mean

Opinionated, blunt, challenging, rude.

Inspirational
Does mean

We are positive, passionate, uplifting in the promotion of a healthy lifestyle.

Doesn't mean

Heady, over excited, glorifying.

Disciplined
Does mean

We are systematic, hardworking, diligent.

Doesn't mean

Being fixed to one way of doing things, quiet and obeying, bland.

Promise Dimensions
(The three most important aspects including objectives and activities to consistently deliver and bring your Promise 'to life' for customers.)

Fresh and tasty organics
Which means

Customers experience superior quality and fresh taste every time.

Each store's display is always beautifully presented and staff take every care to minimise perishable nature of products.

Reassurance of ethical standards from customers knowing who suppliers are and how they produce the food they eat.

Touchpoint action
- Staff Induction Manual
- Presentation/storage training
- 'Farm to Plate' reporting
- Machinery calibration
- Monthly supplier meetings
- 'Meet supplier' in store
- Test & Measure procedures

Inspirational organic knowledge
Which means

Customers find a wealth of interesting and informative content about our local suppliers, our processes and organics health benefits, in store and online.

We are knowledgable and love to answer questions and advise our customers.

We embrace the organic way and help our customers revitalise eating habits.

Touchpoint action
- Point of sale information
- Instore organic library/recipes
- Blog, ePapers/Whitepapers
- Staff training on trends, facts, misnomers
- Nuture partnerships

Easy access to organics
Which means

Customers get 100% fresh, organic and food delivered 7 days a week in all major capitals in Australia through online store.

Touchpoint action
- Website store
- Delivery van graphics
- Recycle/return boxes
- Loyalty Program

Your brand foundations

"Think like a wise man but communicate in the language of the people." – William Butler Yeats

The ball is in your court now. When you finish working through all of the seven steps you will be the proud owner of a new brand. Use the foundations you create to encourage someone to buy your product or service, and use it to support whatever sales or marketing activities you deem appropriate.

Your brand foundations don't explicitly say, "buy me," instead, they say, "This is what I am. This is why I exist. If you agree, if you like me, you can buy me, support me, and recommend me to your friends."

Above all, remember:

Branding is strategic; it's the creation of something worth demanding.

Marketing on the other hand is tactical; it's the generation of demand.

Marketing may contribute to a brand, but your brand is bigger than any particular marketing effort. Your brand is what remains after the marketing has swept through the room. It's the association that sticks in your customers mind after they experience your product, service, or organization—whether or not, at that particular moment, they bought or did not buy.

Your brand ultimately determines if your prospects will become loyal customers or not. Your marketing may convince them to buy from you, but it is your brand that will determine if they buy from you for the rest of their lives.

The foundations you build by following the steps in this book, or by using my recently released Plan2Brand eTool (www.plan2brand. com.au), will help you:

Grow their brand more rapidly

With solid and strategic foundations in place, and by targeting clear market segments, Leaf's focused efforts will enable them to grow their brand faster than if they use the 'throw mud on the wall and see what sticks' approach.

Attract more loyal customers

By understanding the problems and issues their clients are experiencing, and demonstrating that they have the solutions to support them in overcoming these problems, they will quickly build loyalty and create advocates for their brand.

Become the clear choice and beat their competitors

By creating a distinct and sustainable competitive advantage, Leaf's brand will cut through the noise and be remembered for its uniqueness, even in a competitive marketplace.

Build a website customers will love

Clarity and focus on their point of difference, their target market and their brand personality puts them into the driver's seat so they can create bulletproof briefs for web developers and copywriters.

Create powerful, clear and consistent messages

Having a clear understanding of what their brand stands for will ensure that everything they write, post and comment on will reinforce their brand's positioning and touch the hearts and minds of their prospects – helping them to stand apart and stand out.

Attract and assemble a great team

With a clear purpose, vision and pillars guiding their brand, they'll attract team members who believe what they believe and who will feel empowered to make decisions autonomously to support them, multiplying the effectiveness of their efforts.

Grow through better partnerships

A clear focus on the differentiated value their brand delivers and what they are 'bringing to the party' makes attracting partnerships and collaborating easier and more rewarding for everybody involved.

Get a higher ROI on marketing investments

Narrowing their marketing by picking the best segment helps them focus their resources and messages and get the most out of every dollar and hour they invest in promoting the brand.

A final thought

'Brand is the 'f' word of marketing. People swear by it, no one quite understands its significance and everybody would like to think they do it more often than they do.'
– Mark di Soma

I continue to be captivated by the combination of psychology, art and commerce that mix together to define branding, and I hope that my obsession has resulted in a book that goes some way towards changing the way you think about running, and ultimately growing, your business.

I'm leaving you with a few final thoughts.

Be judicious – spending time and money on promoting your business without building foundations strong enough to support your growth is madness. Know your industry, your enemy and your customer better than the competition and you will be better than the competition.

Dare to be different – you may not be the next Google or Amazon in your eyes, but in your customers eyes you can be. Find the courage to go against the tide because the world loves anything new.

Find the fire-in-your-belly – without passion you will not muster the drive to survive. Many of us only get one chance to do it right, so make sure you have enough petrol in the tank.

Above all, think creatively – it's the spark that will set you apart. The combination of creative thinking, creative design and a creative culture leads to endless possibilities.

It's called branding for a reason; make your mark.

Oh, and when you're rich and famous, think of this book and me and drop me a line so I know my passion has ignited your passion.

Your quick-start guide: 22 ways to differentiate

'When positioning a brand, aggressively avoid becoming a 'me too' by assertively being a 'who else?' – Crystal Black Davis

So we've touched on a lot of theory and looked at many examples and many of you will be looking at the worksheets and I'm sure you're thinking by now 'this no easy task.' You're right, and I know you're impatient to grow your business and take over the world – today! So to get you started, here are 22 strategies you might be able to adopt, or even combine, to create a strong point of difference.

Remember, a successful differentiator must meet four important criteria:

- It must be unique to your industry.

- It must be true and provable.

- It must be important enough to be memorable.

- It must be something your prospects desire.

1.   Specialisation. Narrowing your focus and specialising in fewer, or even one industry is not only one of the easiest ways to differentiate, it is potentially the most effective. Building and demonstrating expertise in a smaller niche is highly valued by clients.

2. Leverage a major achievement. Many brands have been built on high-profile achievements. Can you claim you invented a process or a popular app? Preferably something that solved a problem in your industry or solved a problem for a notable client or business.

3. Look or act differently from all of your competitors. A quick look at any industry shows that the majority of companies look and present themselves in almost identical ways. Combine some of your other differentiators with a new look and feel to stand apart.

4. Specialise in offering a specific service. Unique, uncommon or hard-to-find service offerings are often winners. Be conscious of the fact that others might jump on your bandwagon, which would mean your service is no longer differentiated. Address this by emphasising that you were first to market the service.

5. Provide a unique process or truly different way of solving an old problem. Inventing and owning such a process that is truly a game changer.

6. Target a unique audience. A key differentiator for some firms is their in-depth understanding of a particular audience. Your firm might specialise in marketing to Baby Boomer women. Your clients might be retirement planners, insurance companies, or clothing retailers, for example.

7. Provide services to businesses of a certain size. This may not appear to be a sound differentiator, but it is very common. Solo practitioners have a totally different set of needs from multi-nationals. An accountancy firm that serves clients of all sizes is at a distinct advantage to somebody who specialises in only one.

8. Specialise in solving specific business problems. The client or the industry is not relevant here, it's the business challenge they are facing. Often it's something they don't face every day or week and challenges them, such as providing a tender writing and formatting.

9. Develop the skills to become a visible expert in your field, or employ an expert. Having an industry expert leading your team is a great strategy that can be leveraged in a multiple of ways.

10. Create a different business model. Consider moving from billing by the hour to fixed fee or fixed fee by installments. Or offer better credit terms or easy, long-term payment options. This potentially saves time for both your client and yourself. A different business model can be easy to prove and attractive to customers.

11. Offer a guarantee. This is often overlooked but it can be very powerful in reducing the perceived risk to the buyer, especially for online businesses. There are many ways to offer a guarantee. Consider reducing restrictions or conditions, price matching, guaranteeing results or offering a money-back guarantee. To find a guarantee unique to your business think about the good things that happen when customers use your products. Better relationships? More money? Reduced stress? Write down the answer in specific detail, and then guarantee that outcome.

12. Have an unbeatable range. While common in B2C, it's not so common in B2B. Is your selection the broadest? Do you carry more stock or inventory? Is a wide product selection instantly available?

13. Specialise in providing a service or role within a sector or industry. By combining your expertise with an industry focus

you're perceived as different and more qualified. For instance, if you design websites, you can specialise in developing websites for doctors, builders, schools or photographers. The list is endless.

14. Offer a specialised set of resources no one else provides. There is money in intelligence and data, and access to certain information can be a valuable differentiator. Can you create reports, define industry trends or provide statistics that are valuable?

15. Provide access to unique contacts, people or groups. Instead of data or information, offer access to people your prospects want to work or network with. For instance, business-networking hubs sometimes offer access to leading entrepreneurs.

16. Provide an outstanding level of service. Most people claim to offer good service, but many fail to deliver. To rely on your service level as a clear differentiator, it will have to be outstanding.

17. Differentiate yourself by associating with the best. There are a number of ways to do this. For example, showcase the fact that you have a great client list; only work with premium suppliers or only use the best ingredients.

18. Differentiate through size. Large does not have to mean huge; it's all-relative. Size sends a positive signal and as long as you're big in your industry you can create the impression you're also the best.

19. Build a team with a unique combination of expertise. Like a great recipe, a group of employees with a unique set of talents makes an unbeatable team. As a differentiator you're almost capable of defining a new niche within your industry if you communicate it and position yourself that way.

20. Develop partners or strategic relationships. There are many ways to leverage official or semi-official partnerships as a point of difference. Demonstrating that you work closely with respected leaders adds to your credibility.

21. Differentiate by developing the ability to produce a measurable result. This can be easier for an SEO firm that can demonstrate a measurable result, but in practice it can be tricky for many B2Bs. The brand promise exercise can help here.

22. Work only with firms that share a common trait. By focusing on a client's trait or characteristic, instead of their industry or role, you create a competitive advantage. For example, you could provide expatriates with immigration advice. It won't matter what country, industry or role that have.

Peter Engelhardt

Brand Strategist, Entrepreneur, Speaker, Author

Peter Engelhardt is a brand consultant and entrepreneur focused on strategic branding and design for small to medium sized enterprises. He is the founder and driving force behind Creative Brew.

Peter works directly with entrepreneurs and business creators who want to transform their businesses into industry leading brands. To help his clients stand out in an increasingly noisy marketplace, Peter and his team have developed the world's only interactive eTool, Plan2Brand (www.plan2brand.com).

The platform teaches users the concept of strategic branding and provides step-by-step instructions and tools to guide users through the process of building their brand foundations and create a strategic plan.

Over the past 30 years Peter has worked with a long list of highly respected Australian brands. He has travelled extensively throughout Europe and Asia and increasingly is taking advantage of today's technology, working remotely and continuing to grow his business, workshops and speaking engagements.

He lives in Melbourne, Australia with his wife and daughter.